T0301955

MACAT

An Analysis of

Chinua Achebe's

An Image of Africa
Racism in Conrad's
Heart of Darkness

Clare Clarke

Published by Macat International Ltd
24:13 Coda Centre, 189 Munster Road, London SW6 6AW.

Distributed exclusively by Routledge
2 Park Square, Milton Park, Abingdon, Oxon OX14 4RN
711 Third Avenue, New York, NY 10017, USA

Routledge is an imprint of the Taylor & Francis Group, an informa business

www.macat.com
info@macat.com

Cataloguing in Publication Data
A catalogue record for this book is available from the British Library.
Library of Congress Cataloguing-in-Publication Data is available upon request.
Cover illustration: Capucine Deslouis

ISBN 978-1-912302-80-2 (hardback)
ISBN 978-1-912127-77-1 (paperback)
ISBN 978-1-912281-68-8 (e-book)

Notice
The information in this book is designed to orientate readers of the work under analysis,
to elucidate and contextualise its key ideas and themes, and to aid in the development
of critical thinking skills. It is not meant to be used, nor should it be used, as a
substitute for original thinking or in place of original writing or research. References and
notes are provided for informational purposes and their presence does not constitute
endorsement of the information or opinions therein. This book is presented solely for
educational purposes. It is sold on the understanding that the publisher is not engaged
to provide any scholarly advice. The publisher has made every effort to ensure that
this book is accurate and up-to-date, but makes no warranties or representations with
regard to the completeness or reliability of the information it contains. The information
and the opinions provided herein are not guaranteed or warranted to produce particular
results and may not be suitable for students of every ability. The publisher shall not be
liable for any loss, damage or disruption arising from any errors or omissions, or from
the use of this book, including, but not limited to, special, incidental, consequential or
other damages caused, or alleged to have been caused, directly or indirectly, by the
information contained within.

CONTENTS

THE MACAT LIBRARY

The Macat Library is a series of unique academic explorations of seminal works in the humanities and social sciences – books and papers that have had a significant and widely recognised impact on their disciplines. It has been created to serve as much more than just a summary of what lies between the covers of a great book. It illuminates and explores the influences on, ideas of, and impact of that book. Our goal is to offer a learning resource that encourages critical thinking and fosters a better, deeper understanding of important ideas.

Each publication is divided into three Sections: Influences, Ideas, and Impact. Each Section has four Modules. These explore every important facet of the work, and the responses to it.

This Section-Module structure makes a Macat Library book easy to use, but it has another important feature. Because each Macat book is written to the same format, it is possible (and encouraged!) to cross-reference multiple Macat books along the same lines of inquiry or research. This allows the reader to open up interesting interdisciplinary pathways.

To further aid your reading, lists of glossary terms and people mentioned are included at the end of this book (these are indicated by an asterisk [*] throughout) – as well as a list of works cited.

Macat has worked with the University of Cambridge to identify the elements of critical thinking and understand the ways in which six different skills combine to enable effective thinking.
Three allow us to fully understand a problem; three more give us the tools to solve it. Together, these six skills make up the **PACIER** model of critical thinking. They are:

ANALYSIS – understanding how an argument is built
EVALUATION – exploring the strengths and weaknesses of an argument
INTERPRETATION – understanding issues of meaning

CREATIVE THINKING – coming up with new ideas and fresh connections
PROBLEM-SOLVING – producing strong solutions
REASONING – creating strong arguments

To find out more, visit **WWW.MACAT.COM.**

CRITICAL THINKING AND AN IMAGE OF AFRICA

Primary critical thinking skill: CREATIVE THINKING
Secondary critical thinking skill: INTERPRETATION

Few works of scholarship have so comprehensively recast an existing debate as Chinua Achebe's essay on Joseph Conrad's *Heart of Darkness*. Achebe – a highly distinguished Nigerian novelist and university teacher – looked with fresh eyes at a novel that was set in Africa, but in which Africans appear only as onlookers or as indistinguishable "savages". Dismissing the prevailing portrayal of Joseph Conrad as a liberal hero whose anti-imperialist views insulated him from significant criticism, Achebe re-cast the Polish author as a "bloody racist" in an analysis so cogent it changed the way in which his discipline looked not only at Conrad, but also at all works with settings indicative of racial conflict.

The creative contribution of Achebe's essay lies in delving far beneath the surface of Conrad's novel; he not only generated new and highly influential hypotheses about the author's modes of thought and motivations, but also redefined the entire debate over *Heart of Darkness*. Just because the novel had been accepted into the "canon", and now falls into the class of "permanent literature", Achebe says, does not mean we should not question it closely – or criticize its author.

ABOUT THE AUTHOR OF THE ORIGINAL WORK

Born in 1930 in British-ruled Nigeria, **Chinua Achebe** was among the most original and remarkable writers and literary figures of twentieth-century Africa. His 1958 novel *Things Fall Apart* has sold eight million copies and was translated into 50 languages. His academic career, above all in America, was no less spectacular. His unapologetic assertion in 1975 that Joseph Conrad's acclaimed 1899 novel *Heart of Darkness* concealed a hitherto unsuspected racism sparked an academic debate that decisively changed the course of what became known as postcolonial theory. To the end of his life in 2013, Achebe remained a passionate advocate for the right of the authentic voice of Africa to be heard.

ABOUT THE AUTHORS OF THE ANALYSIS

Dr Clare Clarke holds a PhD in English literature from Queen's University Belfast, specialising in Victorian literature. She currently teaches nineteenth-century literature at Trinity College Dublin.

ABOUT MACAT

GREAT WORKS FOR CRITICAL THINKING

Macat is focused on making the ideas of the world's great thinkers accessible and comprehensible to everybody, everywhere, in ways that promote the development of enhanced critical thinking skills.

It works with leading academics from the world's top universities to produce new analyses that focus on the ideas and the impact of the most influential works ever written across a wide variety of academic disciplines. Each of the works that sit at the heart of its growing library is an enduring example of great thinking. But by setting them in context – and looking at the influences that shaped their authors, as well as the responses they provoked – Macat encourages readers to look at these classics and game-changers with fresh eyes. Readers learn to think, engage and challenge their ideas, rather than simply accepting them.

'Macat offers an amazing first-of-its-kind tool for interdisciplinary learning and research. Its focus on works that transformed their disciplines and its rigorous approach, drawing on the world's leading experts and educational institutions, opens up a world-class education to anyone.'

Andreas Schleicher
Director for Education and Skills, Organisation for Economic
Co-operation and Development

'Macat is taking on some of the major challenges in university education … They have drawn together a strong team of active academics who are producing teaching materials that are novel in the breadth of their approach.'

Prof Lord Broers,
former Vice-Chancellor of the University of Cambridge

'The Macat vision is exceptionally exciting. It focuses upon new modes of learning which analyse and explain seminal texts which have profoundly influenced world thinking and so social and economic development. It promotes the kind of critical thinking which is essential for any society and economy.
This is the learning of the future.'

Rt Hon Charles Clarke, former UK Secretary of State for Education

'The Macat analyses provide immediate access to the critical conversation surrounding the books that have shaped their respective discipline, which will make them an invaluable resource to all of those, students and teachers, working in the field.'

Professor William Tronzo, University of California at San Diego

WAYS IN TO THE TEXT

KEY POINTS

- Chinua Achebe (1930–2013) was one of the most important and celebrated African writers of the twentieth century.

- Achebe's essay "An Image of Africa: Racism in Conrad's *Heart of Darkness*" was a powerful attack on the Polish British novelist Joseph Conrad's* famed 1899 novel *Heart of Darkness*. Achebe claimed the novel supported colonialism* and imperialism*—political and social philosophies that define empire-building—and had racist undertones.

- The essay challenges the widely held view that Conrad's novel is a masterpiece of anti-colonialist literature—as a result it has become a cornerstone of writing on *Heart of Darkness* and of postcolonial criticism* more generally.

Who Was Chinua Achebe?

Chinua Achebe, the author of "An Image of Africa: Racism in Conrad's *Heart of Darkness*" (1977), was one of the most widely read, studied, and honored African writers of the twentieth century. He was born in colonial Nigeria in 1930 so had firsthand experience of colonialism—the social, political, and economic phenomenon by which several European nations established control over nations in other parts of the world. Nigeria's tribes and territories lived under British control from 1885 until 1960.

Nevertheless, Achebe had a relatively privileged upbringing and education. He was educated at Government College in Umuahia, a renowned institution based on the British private school model. It provided Achebe with a first-rate education but simultaneously opened his eyes to the desire of the colonialists to stifle native language and culture.

Achebe later won a scholarship to study at University College at Ibadan, Nigeria, then an affiliate of the University of London. He began working for the Nigerian Broadcasting Corporation and, during this time, wrote his first novel, *Things Fall Apart* (1958), a story about the effects of colonialism on life in a traditional village life, articulated from an African perspective. *Things Fall Apart* became one of the most important works of African fiction in English and won Achebe international recognition.

Achebe taught at the University of Nigeria and at various North American universities, including the University of Massachusetts. He published a number of highly regarded novels set in Nigeria, as well as numerous influential works of criticism exposing colonialist biases in English fiction. Throughout his career, he argued for the importance of African literature and remained an outspoken public figure on African politics, particularly on the Biafran War* (1967–70), a bloody civil war in which millions of Nigerians died.

Achebe died in 2013 at the age of 82.

What Does "An Image of Africa" Say?

In "An Image of Africa," Achebe proposes that in his critically acclaimed novel *Heart of Darkness*, the Polish British novelist Joseph Conrad fundamentally misrepresents his African characters so that they reinforce perceptions of African people, culture, and environment as savage and prehistoric. The essay, a criticism of the negative representation of Africa in Western culture, was first delivered as a lecture at the University of Massachusetts in February 1975 and subsequently published.

Achebe suggests that, in the West, there is a psychological need to think of Africa in terms of negative opposition to Europe—that is, as a place essentially uncivilized, savage, and bestial. The dominance of these overused categorizations in Western culture in turn serves to reaffirm Europe's status as Africa's opposite: as civilized, refined, and humane.

In order to demonstrate this tendency, Achebe turns to Conrad's novel to expose the author's depiction of African characters as savage and brutal. Through a highly critical reading of *Heart of Darkness*, Achebe identifies the influence of colonialism in Conrad's fiction. Achebe asks his audience to consider whether Conrad's novel promotes racist views of Africa, and to reflect on its wider implications. How can we support and celebrate art that fundamentally dehumanizes people?

The question poses a challenge to a Western audience of ordinary readers and academics invested in the highly regarded works of art that compose the Western canon* (the body of literature considered by scholars to be worthy of academic study and criticism). Achebe suggests that, by not critically considering the racist and colonialist attitudes in classic texts like *Heart of Darkness*, critics and readers are tacitly supporting those attitudes. How, he asks, can a text that circulates racist and colonialist attitudes towards the non-Western world ever be considered a great work of art?

Achebe argues that the racism in Conrad's novel had been overlooked simply because of the quality of Conrad's writing. While Achebe was a great admirer of Conrad, he was troubled by the way his writing concealed damaging representations of Africa and how these had, until then, remained unnoticed in critical assessments. Achebe's text aimed to create a new space that allowed for the critical evaluation of novels such as Conrad's by bringing the issues of race and colonialism to the fore. In this way, he anticipated the burgeoning discipline of postcolonial criticism (a form of cultural criticism that addresses the various legacies of colonialism) and the analysis of the cultural experience of colonization it offers. Furthermore, "An Image of Africa" put forward an alternative narrative of the African continent and its people to counter the one presented by Conrad and the West more widely. The essay has an underlying desire to correct what Achebe saw as mistaken perceptions of Africa and to give African writers their own voice.

Why Does "An Image of Africa" Matter?

With "An Image of Africa," Achebe became the first critic to challenge the consensus that Conrad's *Heart of Darkness* was an important anti-colonialist text and a novel worthy of canonical status. As a result, the essay has come to occupy a significant place amongst works of revisionist literary criticism (that is, works that seek to challenge readings, critical approaches, and assumptions traditionally accepted with little question).

Achebe's singling out of Conrad highlights a wider problem of the representation of Africa in the dominant Western European mindset at the end of the nineteenth century. The essay challenged assumptions about civilization and culture that were embedded in modern critical approaches, and argued against the understanding that the set of ideals advanced in Conrad's book were universal. It was a daring proposition.

"An Image of Africa" is one of the first works to recognize the influence of colonialism on fiction. It is an extremely provocative text and has continued to be divisive and controversial. Since its publication, the author of practically every critical work on Conrad has felt compelled to either agree or take issue with Achebe's views. What is undeniable is the essay's significant place in the roll of literary criticism. In terms of its broader influence upon postcolonial studies and theory, which specifically address the various legacies of colonialism, few postcolonial critics would deny the importance and impact of Achebe's initial critical inquiry, but—as in the realm of literary criticism—not everyone has fully agreed with all its arguments. The postcolonial scholar Edward Said's* *Culture and Imperialism* (1993), for instance, in which Said evaluates various classic works of literature in the light of their responses to colonialism and race, is also critical of Conrad. But Said does not go as far as Achebe; rather more moderately, he suggests that while Conrad's writing employs racial epithets, his views must be understood in the context of dominant and widespread late-Victorian attitudes to race and empire.

The text's enduring importance rests in its fundamental defense of a universal notion of human integrity. "An Image of Africa" is a work that compels us as readers to change our sense of what we are by restoring a sense of humanity, and challenging those narratives that question the humanity of Africans.

SECTION 1
INFLUENCES

MODULE 1
THE AUTHOR AND THE HISTORICAL CONTEXT

KEY POINTS

* Chinua Achebe's criticism of Joseph Conrad's novel *Heart of Darkness* as racist marked a watershed moment in both literary criticism and the development of postcolonial* theory, which critically addresses the legacies of colonialism.*

* Born in Nigeria while the country and its tribes were under British rule, Achebe experienced racism while growing up.

* Achebe's lecture came at a time of increasing political and social upheaval as African nations claimed their independence from the European nations that had colonized them, making Achebe part of the burgeoning scholarly tradition now known as postcolonial theory.

Why Read This Text?

With "An Image of Africa: Racism in Conrad's *Heart of Darkness*," Chinua Achebe became the first critic to challenge the consensus that Joseph Conrad's novel *Heart of Darkness* (1899) was an important anti-colonialist text and a novel worthy of canonical* status—that is, a defining work in the tradition of Western literature. "An Image of Africa" was first delivered as a lecture at the University of Massachusetts in February 1975; an amended version was later published as an essay in *The Massachusetts Review* and in a collection of Achebe's essays titled *Hopes and Impediments* (1988).[1]

Before Achebe's "An Image of Africa," *Heart of Darkness* was regarded as a classic anti-colonialist text. Following a trip to Africa,

15

> **❝** Coming of age in the 1950s during a significant moment between the waning of the traditional and stable Igbo culture, and Nigeria's independence, modernization, fracture and fragmentation, Achebe has endured the disruption of his own life by exile, and witnessed the imprisonment and even death of his friends. But without self-pity or bitterness, he has said that artists 'who live at the crossroads are lucky'. **❞**
> Elaine Showalter, "The Man Booker Prizes"

Conrad was ambivalent about the European colonizing mission on the continent, having witnessed firsthand the dehumanizing effects of colonialism on native populations. In many ways, *Heart of Darkness* is an examination of the effects of colonialism's economic and social exploitation that fundamentally questions European civilization, progress, and even humanity. However, while Achebe agreed that Conrad was critical of colonialism, he went against the prevailing critical opinion and argued that the novelist was in fact "a thoroughgoing racist" in his depiction of Africans.[2] For Achebe, this aspect of Conrad's work had previously been "glossed over"[3] by critics and he asked for Conrad's attitudes to race to be reexamined, particularly given that *Heart of Darkness* was considered to be "among the half-dozen greatest short novels in the English language."[4] Because of its racist characteristics, Achebe suggested that Conrad's novel should cease to be regarded as a prestigious classic. He also boldly suggested that many professors of English and literary critics were, unwittingly or not, guilty of reinforcing and perpetuating racist views.

Achebe's "An Image of Africa" marked a watershed both in literary criticism and the development of postcolonial theory, which is the scholarly response to, and analysis of, the social, political, and cultural legacies of colonialism and imperialism—issues that are central to

Achebe's work. Gayatri Spivak,* a key postcolonial theorist, has called "An Image of Africa" "the first significant essay of postcolonial criticism."[5] Achebe's highly controversial and influential essay has since become a cornerstone not just of critical thinking about Conrad's novel but of postcolonial criticism more generally.

Author's Life

Born in the West African nation of Nigeria in 1930, Achebe experienced colonialism and attendant racism personally. Although brought up in one of the Christian faith's two major branches, having an evangelical Protestant minister for a father, Achebe also had access to and a great interest in the Igbo* culture of south eastern Nigeria. He was educated at Government College in Umuahia, a prestigious institution modeled on elite British private schools and funded by the colonial administration. The school provided Achebe with an excellent education, but it also opened his eyes to the ways in which the colonialists smothered native language and culture. The only language allowed at the school was English, which Achebe saw as a means for colonial administrators to impose their sovereignty over children by making them "put away their different mother tongues and communicate in the language of their colonizers."[6]

Achebe won a scholarship to study at the University College at Ibadan, Nigeria, then an affiliate of the University of London, from which he graduated in 1954. He went on to work for the Nigerian Broadcasting Corporation (NBC) as director of external broadcasting in Lagos, then the nation's capital, where he completed his first novel, *Things Fall Apart* (1958).

Achebe was appointed a senior research fellow at the University of Nigeria in 1967. He subsequently taught at various North American universities, including the University of Massachusetts (UMass), the University of Virginia, University of California Los Angeles (UCLA), Bard College, and Brown. He won numerous scholarly prizes and honors. He was also involved in publishing ventures to promote African writing, most notably from 1962 to 1987 when he was founding editor of the British publisher Heinemann's "African Writers Series," which has issued several hundred titles. In addition, Achebe was an outspoken public figure on African politics, particularly on the Biafran War* (1967–70), where he supported the independence of the state of Biafra from the Nigerian federation.

Author's Background
A period of political and social upheaval followed the wave of decolonization that swept Africa in the 1950s and 1960s, as African nations struggled for independence from the European nations that governed them. This period also saw the emergence of a number of works of criticism that influenced the trajectory of what is now called postcolonial theory, and which influenced Achebe's work, including the Martinique-born thinker Frantz Fanon's* *Black Skin, White Masks* (1952) and *The Wretched of the Earth* (1961), and the Tunisian critic Albert Memmi's* *The Colonizer and the Colonized* (1965).

The era in which Achebe's lecture was delivered (the mid-1970s) was a time of political and social upheaval in the United States, marked by the emergence of interrelated political movements intent on challenging dominant ideas about identity, race, gender, and class. In their efforts to promote equality for marginalized identities, movements such as black nationalism* (a political movement that advocated self-determination for Americans of African descent), the feminist* and gay rights* movements, which advocated equal rights for women and homosexuals, and the campaign against the American war in Vietnam* (1955–75) challenged the same kinds of dominant cultural and political ideas that informed late-nineteenth-century imperial discourse (roughly, debates and assumptions, and the language used to conduct them). These movements were slowly starting to penetrate the academic world, as Achebe's presence on the faculty at the University of Massachusetts demonstrates.

NOTES

1   Chinua Achebe, "An Image of Africa: Racism in Conrad's *Heart of Darkness*," *Massachusetts Review* 18, no. 4 (1977): 782–794.

2   Achebe, "An Image of Africa," 12.

3   Achebe, "An Image of Africa," 12.

4   Achebe, "An Image of Africa," 16.

5   Gayatri Chakravorty Spivak, "A Moral Dilemma," in *What Happens to History: The Renewal of Ethics in Contemporary Thought*, ed. Howard Marchitello (New York: Routledge, 2001), 234.

6   Ezenwa-Oheato, *Chinua Achebe: A Biography* (Oxford: James Currey, 1997), 30.

MODULE 2
ACADEMIC CONTEXT

KEY POINTS

- Joseph Conrad's* *Heart of Darkness* was inspired by the author's negative experience as a merchant sailor on the Congo River.
- Achebe believed Conrad's novel occupied a privileged place in writing about Africa.
- Early classroom encounters with literature about Africa sparked off Achebe's thinking about race and colonial history that would later influence his writing—and which would in turn become central to postcolonial* critical thought.

The Work in its Context

When considering Chinua Achebe's "An Image of Africa: Racism in Conrad's *Heart of Darkness*" in context, it is more important to position it in relation to the culture—and the particular representative of that culture—that he was writing against than to place it in any academic field. Achebe's criticism was first and foremost directed at the cultural, educational, and intellectual institutions that propagated the heritage of colonialism. Central to this heritage was a pervasive liberal idea—an idea founded on a political philosophy that emphasizes individuality and personal liberty—that the world could be put right through human effort. This idea underlines the colonial experience that led directly to the novel that inspired Achebe's response, Joseph Conrad's *Heart of Darkness*.

Before turning to writing, Conrad had spent years as a sailor in the French and British merchant navies. In 1890 he was appointed captain

> ❝ They howled and leaped, and spun, and made horrid faces; but what thrilled you was just the thought of their humanity—like yours—the thought of your remote kinship with this wild and passionate uproar. Ugly. ❞
>
> Joseph Conrad, *Heart of Darkness*

of a Belgian riverboat on the Congo River in Africa. Encountering frequent looting and terrible treatment of the native population, the experience was overwhelmingly negative. It continued to weigh on Conrad's mind and shaped *Heart of Darkness*, which he wrote 10 years after his trip.

The novel is narrated by English seaman Charles Marlow, also the authors alter-ego.* Employed by a Belgian organization to captain a riverboat on the Congo, Marlow travels to meet a mysterious ivory trader named Kurtz; en route, he witnesses the brutal treatment of natives at the organization's outposts. The cruelty he experiences leads to a fundamental questioning of the nature of European imperialism* in Africa but, more deeply, it also forces Marlow to examine man's capacity for barbarity towards his fellow human beings.

In *Heart of Darkness*, Conrad takes on this question of human barbarity, and the novel develops a compelling series of comparisons between civilization and savagery, between light and darkness. White travelers and settlers, as much as native Africans, are capable of unspeakable acts of cruelty that plunge the human soul into darkness. On one level, the novel criticizes imperialism as being predicated upon acts of savagery, but similarly the writing of the novel was triggered by the Benin Massacre* of 1897, in which a British mission was slaughtered in Benin, west Africa. In the novel, reports of African barbarism abound, culminating in Kurtz's report for the International Society for the Suppression of Savage Customs, in which he recommends: "Exterminate all the brutes!"

Overview of the Field

The novel's journey of discovery has been read as a critique of Western imperialism just as this social and historical phenomenon was nearing its peak. Achebe challenges this, however, criticizing the work's morality over its aesthetic merits, and arguing that it celebrates the dehumanization of the human race. *Heart of Darkness* carries a significant symbolic significance for Achebe, as he felt personally challenged by the text. Both *Heart of Darkness* and Conrad himself occupied privileged places in European writing about Africa. Critics such as the American thinker James Clifford praised Conrad as an admirable anthropologist and his work as a model of ethnography for representing "a subjective position and a historical site of narrative authority that truthfully juxtaposes different truths."[1]

It was this revered status that Achebe found particularly problematic. He explains that "Conrad ... is undoubtedly one of the great stylists of modern fiction and a good storyteller into the bargain. His contribution therefore falls automatically into a different class—permanent literature—read and taught and constantly evaluated by serious academics."[2] Following its inclusion in the influential British literary critic F. R. Leavis's* *The Great Tradition* (1948), Conrad's novel was considered by scholars of literature to occupy an important place within the canon* of great English literature, and Conrad came to be named as one of the tradition's greatest and most important novelists. In his discussion of Conrad's novel, however, Leavis does not mention the novel's imperialist context. Achebe felt that this kind of omission was symptomatic of the novel's place in the canon, which was "so secure" that it existed in a place that shielded it from critical reassessment.[3] Only from this point, from a position of untouchability, was it possible to question the entire construction and preservation of the canon of high literature.

Academic Influences

A series of intellectual encounters experienced by Achebe were more significant in the shaping of "An Image of Africa" than direct academic influences. In his memoirs, Achebe describes his realization that his schoolboy interpretation of Conrad's novel had been wrong. He was horrified by his new understanding of the novel's representations of race: "I did not see myself as an African in those books. I took sides with the white men against the savages ... The savages arrayed against him were sinister and stupid, never anything higher than cunning. I hated their guts. But a time came when I reached the appropriate age and realized that these writers had pulled a fast one on me! I was not on Marlow's boat steaming up the Congo in *Heart of Darkness*; rather, I was one of those unattractive beings jumping up and down on the riverbank, making horrid faces."[4]

Achebe's later experiences at University College in the southern Nigerian city of Ibadan were highly formative for him, particularly for his future career as a writer. Neither Africa nor African humanity were central subjects of critical study in any of the courses Achebe studied for his humanities degree. Indeed, Achebe has suggested that driving his desire to become a novelist and critic was in part his experience in a classroom confrontation over the Anglo-Irish novelist Joyce Cary's* *Mister Johnson* (1939), a novel dealing with Nigeria's colonial regime. Achebe was infuriated by the perspective on his homeland, which he believed to be Eurocentric* (written with the assumption that its audience shared its European sensibilities and focus). "*Mister Johnson* ... was praised so much, and it was clear to me that this was a most superficial picture not only of the country, but even of the Nigerian character and so I thought if this was famous, then perhaps someone ought to try and look at this from the inside."[5]

These classroom encounters with literature about Africa seem to have sparked off the thinking that led to Achebe's composition of "An Image of Africa." The desire to look from the inside is the driving force in both his reading and writing. He sets out to engage in an entirely new way of reading critically against these discourses and his eventual aim is to give shape through writing to a counter-reality that stands against the version of the reality of African that had been disseminated for so long.

NOTES

1   James Clifford, *The Predicament of Culture* (Cambridge, MA: Harvard University Press, 1988), 99.

2   Chinua Achebe, "An Image of Africa: Racism in Conrad's *Heart of Darkness,*" *Massachusetts Review* 18, no. 4 (1977): 783.

3   Achebe, "An Image of Africa," 783.

4   Chinua Achebe, *The Education of a British-Protected Child* (London: Penguin, 2011), 87.

5   Chinua Achebe, in Dennis Duerden and Cosmo Pieterse, eds, *African Writers Talking: A Collection of Interviews* (London: Heinemann, 1972), 4.

MODULE 3
THE PROBLEM

KEY POINTS

- The core question Chinua Achebe addresses is whether a text that reproduces (and implicitly promotes) colonialist* and racist attitudes towards the non-Western world can ever be considered great.

- At the time of Achebe's lecture, several African writers were beginning to examine the experience of colonization in Africa.

- Achebe's work occupies an important place in revisionist literary criticism (i.e., literary criticism that challenges orthodox assumptions).

Core Question

In "An Image of Africa: Racism in Conrad's *Heart of Darkness*," Chinua Achebe asks his audience to consider whether Joseph Conrad's* 1899 novel *Heart of Darkness* is racist. He asks readers to examine the ways in which Conrad presents Africa and Africans and evaluate these representations for racist and colonialist attitudes. Achebe also asks his audience to reassess the inclusion of *Heart of Darkness* in the Western canon.* Achebe's central claim takes the form of a challenge, asking his Western audience to consider "whether a novel which celebrates this dehumanization, which depersonalizes a portion of the human race, can be called a great work of art."[1]

Achebe's answer to this question is powerful and definitive: "No, it cannot. I would not call that man an artist, for example, who composes an eloquent instigation to one people to fall upon another and destroy them. No matter how striking his imagery or how beautiful his

> ❝ *Heart of Darkness* projects the image of Africa as 'the other world,' the antithesis of Europe and therefore of civilization, a place where man's vaunted intelligence and refinement are finally mocked by triumphant bestiality. ❞
>
> Chinua Achebe, "An Image of Africa: Racism in Conrad's *Heart of Darkness*"

cadences fall such a man is no more a great artist than another may be called a priest who reads the mass backwards or a physician who poisons his patients."[2]

Although Achebe admires Conrad's writing, he proposes that what ultimately counts is more than a simple question of aesthetics (that is, the surface properties that might be considered "beautiful" or "ugly"). For Achebe, this is a question that extends beyond Conrad and the text itself, and concerns Western academia more widely and its literary establishment. It is not so much an assessment of what constitute greatness, as a criticism of the institutions that reproduce (and implicitly promote) colonialist and racist attitudes towards the non-Western world, even as they think they are doing the opposite.

The Participants

"An Image of Africa" is part of a wider body of scholarship addressing the processes of nineteenth-century colonization and mid-twentieth-century decolonization* on native Africans. The questions asked by Achebe can be seen as an extension of the sorts of queries posed by a number of earlier writers on the experiences of being colonized, such as the Martinque-born psychiatrist and cultural critic Frantz Fanon's* *Black Skin, White Masks* (1952) and *The Wretched of the Earth* (1961), and the Tunisian thinker Albert Memmi's* *The Colonizer and the Colonized* (1965). For instance, Achebe's analysis of the West's imagination of Africa as a negative projection of itself draws on the psychoanalytic* model of colonialism proposed by Fanon, to argue that European depictions of colonies as the "Other" are symptomatic of the West's own cultural neuroses.

Achebe built on Fanon's application of a "moral dualism" to colonial relations. To explain, the philosophical term "Manichaean dualism" describes the belief that an action or a state might be either "good" or "evil." For Fanon, the experience of colonization was constructed in these terms, with an essential opposition between the colonizer and the colonized, in which each group is respectively set up as "self" and "Other," white and black, and—finally—good and evil.

Fanon's *The Wretched of the Earth*, written at the time of the Algerian* struggle for independence from colonial rule, explores the psychological effects of colonization on the colonized people. Fanon criticizes the African nationalist Leopold Senghor's* vision of an independent Africa, arguing that it is still entangled in European colonial terms. Fanon believes that, contrary to his purpose, Senghor has accepted the basic premise of colonization—the inferiority of the colonized—and that this is an unacceptable point from which to form a collective sense of national African identity. Fanon proposes instead that any attempt to redress colonial discourse must be carried out on its own terms, not by engaging with—and therefore giving credibility to—ideas received from Europeans.

The Contemporary Debate

The purpose of Fanon's criticism of Senghor is to show us how negative views of Africa are deeply embedded—even those from an African perspective—when filtered through European expectations. At the time Senghor was living in Paris and Fanon suggested that this shaped his perception of Africa, even of his own identity. The main question he asked was, therefore, is it possible to discover a truthful African identity through a European perspective?

While Achebe shared this preoccupation with Fanon, his approach was more academic than political. If the most important literary texts that explore the questions of African experience and identity—in this case, Conrad's novel—present a fundamentally negative view, what is the consequence for African readers? How does this affect the formation of their own identity and feelings of worth if the only notable representations they have of themselves are as subjugated peoples?

Texts like Fanon's and Achebe's brought about a fundamental questioning of the Western canon that would undermine its former preeminence. More importantly, it was also being cast in a new light. Following these developments, the canon could no longer be represented as a repository of high values once these had been connected to a history of imperial violence and racism.

Scholars began to concentrate on the fact that many great works of art and literature advanced negative attitudes towards certain geographic regions and ethnic groups. Works such as the Caribbean novelist Jean Rhys's* *Wide Sargasso Sea* (1966) anticipated "An Image of Africa" by brightly illuminating the racism implicit in the British novelist Charlotte Brontë's* novel *Jane Eyre* (1847), and arguing that such novels created the cultural preconditions necessary for both enabling and sustaining the British empire. Rhys rewrote the life of Bertha, a creole woman (that is, a woman of mixed European and black descent) described in animalistic and villainous terms in Brontë's novel, in order to give her story a voice of her own. The wider implication is to give Caribbean people—and, by extension, any people with a history of being colonized—the opportunity to tell their own story and narrate their own history, rather than simply inherit versions of their lives as seen in colonial narratives.

NOTES

1   Chinua Achebe, "An Image of Africa: Racism in Conrad's *Heart of Darkness*," *Massachusetts Review* 18, no. 4 (1977): 788.

2   Achebe, "An Image of Africa," 788–789.

MODULE 4
THE AUTHOR'S CONTRIBUTION

KEY POINTS

- Chinua Achebe aimed to challenge the critical consensus of Joseph Conrad's* novel *Heart of Darkness* by exposing its racist tendencies.

- To undermine the negative image of Africa portrayed by Conrad, Achebe constructed Africa as a real place with a sophisticated history.

- Achebe built on work on the phenomenon of decolonization to question the formation of cultural canons* (traditions in which certain artistic productions are awarded a particular status).

Author's Aims

Chinua Achebe's "An Image of Africa: Racism in Conrad's *Heart of Darkness*" was intended to urge critics, students, and educators to consider the representation of Africa and African people in literature and to recognize the influence of colonial* ideology on fiction. It aims to encourage the questioning of assumptions about Africa prevalent in European thought by forcefully challenging the critical consensus of Conrad's *Heart of Darkness* as an important anti-colonialist text. Achebe proposes that Conrad's celebrated critique of imperialism* is flawed, suggesting that it is still rooted in discourses that call attention to racial difference between white and black. He argues that "Conrad saw and condemned the evil of imperial exploitation but was strangely unaware of the racism on which it sharpened its iron tooth."[1] Achebe thus places Conrad firmly on the side of racism: the fundamental idea sustaining all colonialism.

❝ Sometimes his [Conrad's] fixation on blackness is truly overwhelming. **❞**

Chinua Achebe, "An Image of Africa: Racism in Conrad's *Heart of Darkness*"

Achebe is relentless in his criticism of Conrad, and does not even concede that he can be forgiven for reflecting the social views of a bygone era. He cites contemporaries of Conrad's such as the Spanish artist Pablo Picasso* and the French artists Henri Matisse* and Maurice de Vlaminck* to contrast their views. Achebe recalls Vlaminck receiving an African mask made by the Fang tribe—a native people living just north of the Congo River—in 1905, and subsequently showing it to Matisse, the sculptor André Derain,* and Picasso, all of whom were "greatly affected by it."[2] For Achebe, this mask illustrates that the native people living around the Congo in the late-nineteenth century were much more highly evolved and cultured than Conrad allows. But more importantly, this anecdote serves to illustrate that Conrad's negative depiction of Africa and Africans was not innocent. Achebe wants to show that Conrad chose Africa because it could be represented as an antithetical (that is, an opposite and negative) image of Europe and its perceived idea of civilization. Achebe's object of criticism is, therefore, much bigger than just Conrad himself: it is the institutions, ideologies, and beliefs of Western culture. He aims, in essence, to tear apart Western knowledge of the rest of the world and the ways in which the West comes to know other people and other cultures.

Approach

In order to expose Conrad as a racist, Achebe sets out to undermine Conrad's readings of Africa as truthful. Achebe does not so much perform a close critical reading of *Heart of Darkness* as simply allow Conrad's views about Africa to speak for themselves. He is systematic and logical in his approach. First, he suggests that Conrad reduces Africa to a mere backdrop against which to stage a solely European story, in which only European characters play roles of any significance. Achebe suggests that both the African geography and its people are represented as another world, and that this depiction is empty and vague, without any truthful substance. To counter this ornamental representation of Africa, Achebe articulates a vision of Africa in which it becomes a real place again, not simply a prop that supports a story for the audience in another place.

The process begins by subverting the metaphors in Conrad's title. Conrad's "Heart"—which can be read as an essence, or essential understanding, of Africa—is replaced by "Image," which calls attention to its status as a representation and, thus, an artificial construction. Similarly, the abstract "Darkness" becomes a concrete place, "Africa." In this way, Achebe turns the symbolic back into the real place from which Conrad created his inauthentic, biased, and unrepresentative image. It is an image that, in Achebe's eyes, "amounts to no more than a steady, ponderous, fake-ritualistic repetition of two sentences, one about silence and the other about frenzy."[3] In this way, Achebe offers an evaluation of how Conrad's representation of Africa and Africans fails to satisfy realistic criteria, and simply reproduces convenient tales that serve to sustain Africa's global position as an inferior backdrop to Europe's civilization.

Contribution in Context

With his lecture and subsequent essay, Achebe challenged many of the prevailing critical opinions on the novel and ideas about the Western canon. It is important to consider Achebe's lecture within its academic context in order to understand just how daring, controversial, and original it was. "An Image of Africa"—delivered in 1975 to an audience of students and faculty staff at the University of Massachusetts—came at a time before non-Western literature was widely studied and postcolonial* approaches taught. Achebe's lecture called into question the utility, and arguably the morality, of the prevailing methods of studying literature and constructing canons. Achebe was also boldly suggesting that many professors of English and literary critics were (albeit unwittingly) guilty of reinforcing and perpetuating racist views. And finally, he was of course criticizing a "classic" of the Western canon, arguing that a text considered anti-colonialist for decades was in fact just the opposite and, moreover, extremely racist.

While undoubtedly an original text, Achebe's lecture nevertheless shared ideas and questions that had been in circulation within scholarship for the previous two decades or so on the processes of colonization and decolonization* (the works of Frantz Fanon,* for example). Later, however, *Heart of Darkness* had come to be regarded as a key anti-colonialist text. In *The Political Novels of Joseph Conrad* (1963), literary critic Eloise Knapp Hay reads the novel as "a vehement denunciation of imperialism and racism."[4] Another literary critic, Arnold Kettle, went even further, suggesting that it is "perhaps the most horrifying description of imperialism ever written."[5]

NOTES

1   Chinua Achebe, "An Image of Africa: Racism in Conrad's *Heart of Darkness*," *Massachusetts Review* 18, no. 4 (1977): 794.

2   Frank Willett, quoted by Achebe, "An Image of Africa," 791.

3   Achebe, "An Image of Africa," 783–784.

4   Eloise Knapp Hay, *The Political Novels of Joseph Conrad* (Chicago: Chicago University Press, 1963), 112.

5   Arnold Kettle, *An Introduction to the English Novel*, vol. 2 (London: Hutchinson, 1953), 64.

SECTION 2
IDEAS

MODULE 5
MAIN IDEAS

KEY POINTS

- The key themes in "An Image of Africa" are the need for those in the West to set up Africa and Europe as opposites; Joseph Conrad's* racism; and the questioning of the Western canon.*

- Achebe's overall argument is the apparent need in the West to see Africa as inherently uncivilized and bestial so as to shore up Western notions of itself as civilized and refined.

- "An Image of Africa" is tightly focused on its aims and does not stray far from the main subject. The result is a deeply personal, passionate, and provocative piece of writing.

Key Themes

In "An Image of Africa: Racism in Conrad's *Heart of Darkness*," Chinua Achebe proposes that in Western societies there is a need to conceive of Africa as inherently uncivilized and bestial in order to reinforce Europe's idea of itself as civilized and refined. In other words, Achebe argues that the book sets up a view of Africa as a psychological opposite against which Europe can be measured to its advantage. Achebe turns to Joseph Conrad's novel *Heart of Darkness* to illustrate this tendency, exposing Conrad's portrayal of natives as savage and brutal.

Achebe's argument is brought together by several key themes. First, the apparent need for many in the West to portray Africa and Europe as opposing entities comprising different values. Second, Conrad's own racism, as demonstrated by his dehumanization of the African characters in the novel, and the broader implications of the tacit acceptance of commonplace racism of this kind within the Western

> ❝ It is the desire—one might indeed say the need—in Western psychology to set Africa up as a foil to Europe, a place of negations at once remote and vaguely familiar in comparison with which Europe's own state of spiritual grace will be manifest. ❞
>
> Chinua Achebe, "An Image of Africa: Racism in Conrad's *Heart of Darkness*"

canon. Third, the question of whether a work of literature that dehumanizes a whole section of the human race should be considered a great work of art. And finally, the extent to which attitudes to race in works such as Conrad's need to be recognized and redressed.

Exploring the Ideas

"An Image of Africa" begins with an anecdote about how a number of people whom Achebe has encountered have expressed surprise that African literature is studied at universities in the West. From here, Achebe goes on to state that he believes this is because of a prevailing Western assumption that measures Africa only in relation to Europe—Europe as civilized and well-known, and Africa as uncivilized and mysterious. Achebe goes on to argue that he believes Conrad's *Heart of Darkness* provides one of the best illustrations of this tendency. Achebe illustrates his claim that Conrad is a racist with close analysis of the novel's representation of African natives.

For Achebe, Conrad's descriptions rely too heavily on the words "nigger" and "black," and similarly portray Africans as devoid of humanity, often devoid of language.[1] Although Conrad is a product of his time and is critical of imperialism,* Achebe argues that the novelist is blind to his own racism. Achebe goes on to relate this analysis of Conrad to his concern that the novel has been given elevated status as one of the great works of Western literature, claiming that its racist attitudes are not merely condoned but perpetuated. He suggests that these attitudes cannot be overturned easily but closes by expressing the tentative hope that the daunting work of redressing this prejudice will begin soon.

Achebe acknowledges that Conrad was not responsible for his portrayal of African natives as uncivilized. Rather, he employed what "was and is the dominant image of Africa in the Western imagination."[2] Thus, for Achebe, *Heart Of Darkness* frequently employs negative and racist stereotypes in its descriptions of African natives—Conrad depicts the African people as savage, ugly, cannibalistic, inhumane, and without language. For Achebe, *Heart of Darkness* constructs an image of Africa as "the other world" and "the antithesis of Europe and therefore of civilization."[3] Achebe argues that what concerns Conrad is not the difference between Africa and Europe, but rather the similarities: "the lurking hint of kinship" that suggests links between the African natives and contemporary Europeans.[4] Achebe argues that "the West seems to suffer deep anxieties about the precariousness of its civilization and to have a need for constant reassurance by comparing it with Africa."[5] He employs a metaphor to illustrate this claim. As he puts it, "Africa is to Europe as the picture is to Dorian Gray*—a carrier onto whom the master unloads his physical and moral deformities so that he may go forward, erect and immaculate."[6] For Achebe, writing in 1975, this image of Africa still prevailed in Western thought and literature.

The text contains a number of ideas and questions that would become central to later postcolonial criticism.* These are: its contention that Western literature often portrays Africa and Europe as opposing one another and having radically contesting values; its examination of negative representations of non-Western people; and its argument that literary history and literary critics alike have been blind to the importance of race. Taken together, these ideas see Achebe both raising, and beginning to theorize about, the important issue of race in Conrad's work as well as in fiction more broadly.

Language and Expression

In presenting his argument that race is not a marginal or secondary issue but is central to how texts such as *Heart of Darkness* are constructed, Achebe expresses his ideas in simple language free from academic jargon. His points are ordered logically and coherently, and supported by close reference to Conrad's representation of Africa and Africans in the novel. It is a passionate and provocative piece in which, on occasion, Achebe's anger surfaces in violent language that emphasizes the prejudices of the novel, such as his accusation that Conrad was a "bloody racist"[7] or "Conrad had a problem with niggers."[8] The use of these words has a startling impact that creates a palpable sense of discomfort in readers. They call attention to the reader's complicity in Conrad's view by exploiting the idea that the novelist denies a fundamental humanity to his African characters.

It is important to note, however, that Achebe's is an extremely personal response to Conrad's work, presented in an unashamedly subjective manner designed to provoke controversy and debate. It is perhaps the main difficulty in appreciating Achebe's argument. In fact, the essay's deliberately controversial nature is just as likely to alienate as to persuade its audience.

NOTES

1   Chinua Achebe, "An Image of Africa: Racism in Conrad's *Heart of Darkness*," *Massachusetts Review* 18, no. 4 (1977): 789.

2   Achebe, "An Image of Africa," 792.

3   Achebe, "An Image of Africa," 783.

4   Achebe, "An Image of Africa," 783.

5   Achebe, "An Image of Africa," 792.

6   Achebe, "An Image of Africa," 792.

7   This would be changed to "thoroughgoing racist" in later editions.

8   Achebe, "An Image of Africa," 789.

MODULE 6
SECONDARY IDEAS

KEY POINTS

- Achebe draws on the philosophical concept of the "Other" to describe how Africa is portrayed negatively in relation to Europe.

- In his novel *Heart of Darkness*, Joseph Conrad* denies African characters equality by denying them a voice.

- Achebe's essay could be reconsidered in relation to the interest of major European artists of the early twentieth century in the exotic.

Other Ideas 391

One of the key secondary ideas in Chinua Achebe's "An Image of Africa: Racism in Conrad's *Heart of Darkness*" is the representation of a specific ethnic group—indigenous African characters in *Heart of Darkness*—as an "Other." The "Other" is a philosophical notion that comes from the theory of psychoanalysis* referring to that which is separate and distinct from ourselves—something "Other" than and to ourselves. This notion is central to postcolonial* theory, which argues that "Otherness" is deeply embedded in colonial ideologies and forms the basis of all negative racial stereotyping.

The process of "othering" people, places, or cultures is the process of defining them by what they are not, by difference. In this case, imaginary notions of Africa are placed in a discursive relationship—that is, they are co-opted into a "conversation," with all the assumptions and language this requires—with a notion of Europe in which Africa is defined as everything Eurocentrics most fear (black, barbaric, and different), and Europe as everything they hope to be (white, civilized, and familiar).

66 From the beginning of Western speculation about the
Orient, the one thing the Orient could not do was to
represent itself. **99**
Edward Said, *Orientalism*

The African, therefore, is always defined as different from, and in
negative relation to, the European. In this way, the European's presence
in Africa is depicted as a civilizing mission and, in consequence, the
African's natural relation to his or her own home and history is
fractured. A dominant narrative of African relations is imposed on
African lives, ultimately rendering them unworthy.

The consequence of this system of binary oppositions is that
people from colonized nations take on the negative cultural
stereotypes projected on them through works such as Conrad's novel.
Achebe proposes that because works like this carry weight as
authoritative and truthful representations of Africa, African readers
are in danger of accepting its negative representations of African
characters as valid, and consequently of incorporating this negative
understanding of Africa into their own identities.

This type of analysis of the literary and cultural representation of
non-Western cultures has received its fullest treatment in the work of
the Palestinian American cultural critic Edward Said,* who coined
the term "Orientalism"* to describe Western projections onto the
eastern Other. Said's book *Orientalism* (1978) is one of the first full-
length studies of the way Western culture and thought depicts the
Orient. For Said, inaccurate and reductive images of the Orient were
employed by Western society to justify colonialism.

Exploring the Ideas

Achebe explains how this image of Africa as "Other" "was and is the
dominant image of Africa in the Western imagination and that Conrad

merely brought the peculiar gifts of his own mind to bear on it."[1] With this statement, he suggests that in some ways Conrad's novel is not really about Africa, but about Europe's fears about what Africa represents to the collective Western imagination. Paradoxically, this negative conception of Africa gives it tremendous importance and power. More than simple revulsion, the West needs to portray Africa as "Other" to appease its own ambiguous feelings towards the atrocities carried out in the name of what it sought to project as the "civilizing" virtues of colonialism.

One way that Conrad denies Africa its power is by denying Africa a voice in the novel. Achebe suggests that it is "clearly not part of Conrad's purpose to confer language on the 'rudimentary souls' of Africa. They only 'exchanged short grunting phrases' even among themselves but mostly they were too busy with their frenzy."[2] In the few instances in which African characters do speak, their language sets them up as caricatures: the cannibals' "catch 'im ... eat 'im" and the final announcement "Mistah Kurtz—he dead."[3] The imbalance in communication—where only one has the ability to speak at all clearly—troubled Achebe, allowing as it did only one version of Africa to be articulated; moreover, this version effectively silenced anything of value Africa and its people might have had to offer.

In a later essay, Achebe reaffirmed the point: "The white man has been talking and talking and never listening because he imagines he has been talking to a dumb beast."[4] Achebe contends that Conrad does not reveal the truth about the experience of empire in Africa. If anything, he performs the "role of purveyor of comforting myths" about Africa that reaffirm, to paraphrase Achebe, its difference by sidestepping the essential question of equality between white people and black people.[5] To this end, Achebe takes on the role of giving the silenced a voice of their own.

Overlooked

Since "An Image of Africa" is such a short and tightly focused text, practically all of the work advances Achebe's central argument about racism in Conrad's work as well as in Western thought more broadly. Moreover, as the essay is so widely read and studied, essentially all parts of the text have been subjected to intense and detailed critical scrutiny. It is therefore difficult to point out any overlooked elements within it.

Nevertheless, there are some interesting aspects of Achebe's essay that could lead to a broader understanding of the ways in which Western eyes view foreign cultures. In order to counter the idea that African culture is primitive, Achebe briefly expounds the ways in which nineteenth-century African native culture influenced European modernist* art (art of the late nineteenth and early twentieth centuries). Achebe draws attention to the encounter in the early years of the twentieth century between European artists such as Pablo Picasso,* whose contact with an African mask made by the Fang tribe was among many influences on Cubism* (an artistic movement that challenged traditional representations of perspective and geometry in painting and sculpture). Although Achebe focuses on Conrad, the essay poses a broader question: do the dialogues between artists such as Picasso and Africa constitute a kind of colonial exchange that repeats and strengthens imperialist* ideologies of race and empire? Or were there those in Europe, artists above all, who recognized that Africa could contribute decisively to a new, actively modern art? It is a question ripe for further exploration.

NOTES

1   Chinua Achebe, "An Image of Africa: Racism in Conrad's *Heart of Darkness*," *Massachusetts Review* 18, no. 4 (1977): 792.

2   Achebe, "An Image of Africa," 786.

3   Joseph Conrad, quoted in Achebe, "An Image of Africa," 786.

4   Chinua Achebe, *Times Literary Supplement*, February 1, 1980, 113.

5   Achebe, "An Image of Africa," 784.

MODULE 7
ACHIEVEMENT

KEY POINTS

- Achebe's greatest achievement is restoring a sense of confidence in African history.

- The essay helped the rethinking of categories of difference—the ways in which people, cultures, or places are defined with regard to each other—in academic institutions.

- Critics have observed how Achebe can also be accused of racism by privileging non-white readings of Joseph Conrad's* text.

Assessing the Argument

Chinua Achebe's "An Image of Africa: Racism in Conrad's *Heart of Darkness*" marked a turning point in Conrad criticism. Since the essay was published, few new readings of Conrad's novel have failed to address it. It has also contributed significantly to provoking a shift in literary criticism that moves away from questions of the canon*—of placing Conrad firmly in a tradition of great writing—to the convergence of politics and aesthetics in literary texts. Indeed, Achebe's inventive turn was to bring about a wholesale reappraisal of how the "greatness" of literature should be judged.

Overall, the essay's most important achievement is the undermining of a long-held Anglophone view of Africa as savage and dependent on European history, culture, and education. In doing away with this myth, the text restores a sense of humanity, history, and confidence to colonial Africa. As Achebe himself states in a further essay, his aim as a writer is to "teach my readers that their past—with all its

> **❝** The real question is the dehumanization of Africa and Africans which this age-long attitude has fostered and continues to foster in the world. **❞**
>
> Chinua Achebe, "An Image of Africa: Racism in Conrad's *Heart of Darkness*"

imperfections—was not one long night of savagery from which the first European, acting on God's behalf, delivered them."[1] Indeed, the essay succeeds in doing so by appropriating the language of the colonizers and turning it on itself, creating an idiom in the English language that draws from African experience and carries the full weight of its history.

Achievement in Context

It is important to see Achebe's arguments within the context of the North American academic world of the 1970s. This was a period in which psychoanalytic* criticism, feminist* criticism, and New Criticism* (an approach to the analysis of literary texts that emphasized close focus and analysis) dominated literary studies. Achebe's text drew on these schools and anticipated the formation of postcolonial* studies by exploring themes that would eventually form the bedrock of the discipline—namely, the writing of alternative versions of colonial history; the challenge of the psychological construction of colonial subjects as negative "Others"; the questioning of the ideologies of imperialism*; and the challenge to the supposedly universal set of ideals of Western cultural institutions such as the English canon of literature.

The work's provocation was twofold. On one level it was aimed at Conrad's text itself. But it was also directed at an academic world that Achebe considered insulated works like this from contentious readings. As the conclusion of "An Image of Africa" illustrates, Achebe wanted the academic community to become aware of its complicit racism, and to take the necessary courses of action to rectify this problem:"Perhaps a change will come ...There is just the possibility that Western man may begin to look seriously at the achievements of other people ... Although the work which needs to be done may appear too daunting, I believe that it is not one day too soon to begin. And where better than a university?"[2]

However optimistic Achebe's call, critics such as the Conrad scholars Hunt Hawkins* and Cedric Watts* responded to his essay by asserting that his argument was simplistic, accusing him of reducing the complexity of Conrad's work to a question of race.[3] These responses would suggest that Achebe was right to expose the privileged and deep-seated protection that texts like this enjoyed within academia. Indeed, the defense of Conrad by such as Hawkins and Watts highlights precisely Achebe's main point: that defending Conrad on literary grounds was only further reinforcing Conrad's disproportionate view of colonizer and colonized. For this reason, Achebe's essay made a notable contribution to the field of literary criticism. It helped bring about an important rethinking of categories of difference (the way that people or cultures, say, are defined with regard to each other, and the assumptions on which those definitions are founded). Consequently, academic institutions gradually became more familiar with teaching the complex reality of difference in their departments.

Limitations

In "'A Bloody Racist': About Achebe's View of Conrad" (1983), critic Cedric Watts suggests that Achebe's arguments display the type of racism with which he charges Conrad. Watts's essay is one of the most famous rebuttals of Achebe's argument. He contends that Achebe seems to suggest that "whites are disqualified on racial grounds from judging the text."[4] The implication of Watts's argument is that Achebe's position is actively *anti*-universal, separating people into racial groups rather than emphasizing a shared humanity. In this sense Watts's response is just as divisive and polemical as Achebe's original argument. For Achebe, of course, it is Conrad whose text is not universal, and any appearance of universality can arise only from readings that rely on an elite, white, European perspective.

A number of later postcolonial critics and writers from Africa and other former colonies, such as Wilson Harris,* Hunt Hawkins, Frances Singh,* Peter Nazareth,* and Ngugi wa Thiong'o,* have helped to complicate the debate, seeing it as more than simply a face-off between black/white, or occidental/oriental critics. These critics believe that while Conrad was ambivalent on racial matters, his views on race must be understood as a product of the historical context of the late nineteenth century in which the book was written. They argue persuasively that, for his time, Conrad was in fact extremely progressive in his criticism of the colonialists and that this needs to be recognized as the most important feature of the novel. Their opinions help complicate the view that readers' responses to Conrad's novel are largely dependent on their own ethnic background.

NOTES

1   Chinua Achebe, *Morning Yet on Creation Day: Essays* (London: Anchor, 1975), 72.

2   Chinua Achebe, "An Image of Africa: Racism in Conrad's *Heart of Darkness*," *Massachusetts Review* 18, no. 4 (1977): 793–794.

3   See Cedric Watts, "'A Bloody Racist': About Achebe's View of Conrad," *Yearbook of English Studies* 13 (1983): 196–209; and Hunt Hawkins, "The Issue of Racism in *Heart of Darkness*," *Conradiana* 14, no.3 (1982): 163–171.

4   Watts, "'A Bloody Racist'," 96.

MODULE 8
PLACE IN THE AUTHOR'S WORK

KEY POINTS

- Chinua Achebe's body of work is highly unified, focusing on exploring several key themes—particularly the repercussions of intersections between native African culture and colonial rule.

- "An Image of Africa" is a cornerstone of writing on Joseph Conrad's* novel *Heart of Darkness* and of postcolonial* criticism.

- Achebe is not known merely for this essay; his novel *Things Fall Apart*, considered one of the most important works of African literature, is arguably more famous.

Positioning

Chinua Achebe has suggested that his desire to become a novelist and critic—particularly one concerned with the themes found in "An Image of Africa: Racism in Conrad's *Heart of Darkness*"—was in part provoked by his anger at the Eurocentric* perspectives in many literary depictions of Africa and Africans. The types of preoccupations with race and the legacies of colonialism* that inform Achebe's essay can be traced in earlier works such as his first novel, *Things Fall Apart* (1958), which explores the difficult repercussions of intersections between native African culture and colonial rule. Achebe also addressed this subject in an early academic essay, "Colonialist Criticism" (1975), published the same year as his lecture at the University of Massachusetts.

In *Things Fall Apart*, Achebe also explores how Africa's indigenous cultures and sense of history were being displaced and undermined by the experience of colonialism. The novel depicts Umuofia, the

> **❝ Over fifty years, Chinua Achebe's career as a novelist, poet, editor, broadcaster, diplomat, activist, professor, and critic, has been devoted to the circumstances of the African continent. ❞**
> Elaine Showalter, "The Man Booker Prizes"

fictional village where the novel is set, as civilized and sophisticated, challenging the narratives received through a European literary canon* that indoctrinated an understanding of African culture as savage and prehistoric. In doing so, *Things Fall Apart* mounts a similar challenge to the discourses inherited through this canon, and provides an alternative narrative that places Africa at the heart of the colonial exchange and shows Europeans as intrusive outsiders whose presence disrupts African civilization.

Integration

The overall direction of Achebe's intellectual career can be summarized by his aim to show an international audience the inherent richness, complexity, and sophistication in black African literature and culture. *Things Fall Apart* demonstrates the corrosive influence of the European presence in Africa by narrating the gradual dismantling of a traditional African society following the arrival of white Europeans. Here, it is the West that is presented as alien—or "Other"—to African experience, and African values such as community and social contract are emphasized over the reckless, destructive, and foreign individualism of the West.

Achebe also transferred his preoccupation with the consequences of colonial rule on native African culture to his academic life. He was appointed as senior research fellow at the University of Nigeria in 1967, and in 1972 was offered a professorship at the University of Massachusetts. From the outset of his academic career Achebe's scholarly work focused on exposing colonial biases in representations of Africa in Western literature and arguing for the importance of an indigenous African literature. Achebe addressed this subject in an early essay, "Colonialist Criticism" (1975), in which he argues that colonialist biases permeate even sophisticated critical commentary on fiction representing Africa. The extent of Achebe's achievement can be summarized in his appropriation of the English language to forge a new language that refers to Africa in image and tone but carries a universal reach. More than anything else, it is the development of a language that is appropriate to communicate the experience of the African culture that it aims to represent.

Significance

Achebe is one of the best-known African novelists and essayists of his generation. "An Image of Africa" is a cornerstone in his career, of writing on Conrad's novel *Heart of Darkness*, and of postcolonial criticism.* Achebe revisited the topic of racism in Conrad in later academic articles, such as "Africa's Tarnished Name" (1998) and "African Literature as Restoration of Celebration" (1990). In these, Achebe's early views on Conrad and racism in *Heart of Darkness* remain largely unchanged. He continued to make charges of racism against *Heart of Darkness* until his death in 2013, and defended the position he set out in "An Image of Africa."

However, Achebe is perhaps best known to the wider public for his novels. Indeed, *Things Fall Apart* is considered to be one of the most important works of African literature. The text has sold over eight million copies and has been translated into 50 languages, making Achebe the most translated African writer in history. He was also awarded the Man Booker International Prize in 2007, a biennial award in Britain for outstanding achievement in fiction. Achebe's last work, published in October 2012, was *There Was a Country: A Personal History of Biafra*, a memoir in poetry and prose in which Achebe reflects on his experiences of being brought up in colonial Nigeria through to the Biafran Civil War* of the late 1960s. Achebe's outstanding reputation as a thinker and expert in postcolonial criticism remains to the present day.

SECTION 3
IMPACT

MODULE 9
THE FIRST RESPONSES

KEY POINTS

- Achebe was criticized for reproducing racism and for being too extreme in his argument.
- While Achebe did not shy away from addressing his critics, he also did not modify his views in any substantial way.
- No clear critical consensus has been arrived at on the contentious issue of Conrad's* racism, and while few critics would go as far as Achebe in their denunciation of Conrad, fewer still would dispute the import and influence of Achebe's initial critical inquiry.

Criticism

Given the provocative nature of Chinua Achebe's "An Image of Africa: Racism in Conrad's *Heart of Darkness*," it is unsurprising that the essay immediately polarized opinion. Achebe's biographer Ezenwa–Oheato notes how divisive responses began to emerge at the lecture itself from traditional Conrad scholars, who were outraged by his call to remove *Heart of Darkness* from university syllabuses. Oheato narrates how at the reception immediately following his lecture, several professors reacted passionately and emotionally. Achebe was initially reprimanded by the academic community. One professor cried "How dare you!" while another suggested that he had "no sense of humor."[1] Eventually, however, others approached Achebe to make positive remarks, with one scholar admitting that the lecture had made him fundamentally reconsider his views on Conrad: "I now realize that I had never really read *Heart of Darkness* although I have taught it for years."[2]

❝ You see, those who say that Conrad is on my side because he is against colonial rule do not understand that I know who is on my side. And where is the proof that he is on my side? A few statements about it not being a very nice thing to exploit people who have flat noses? This is his defense against imperial control? If so it is not enough. It is simply not enough. If you are going to be on my side what is required is a better argument. Ultimately you have to admit that Africans are people. You cannot diminish a people's humanity and defend them. **❞**

Chinua Achebe, interview in the *Guardian*, 2003

A number of literary critics writing in the years directly following the publication of Achebe's essay, including Susan Blake, Benita Parry,* Eugene B. Redmond,* and Bette London,* agreed with Achebe's argument that *Heart of Darkness* reinforces and reproduces racism.[3] Others have suggested that Achebe's view contained elements of truth but was too extreme. Writers such as Wilson Harris,* Hunt Hawkins,* Frances Singh,* Peter Nazareth,* and Ngugi wa Thiong'o* believed that Conrad's opinions had to be understood as a product of their historical context. Sarvan, Singh, Nazareth, Harris, and Thiong'o's responses are reprinted in the 1988 Norton critical edition of *Heart of Darkness*.

The most famous counter-attack directed at Achebe was in Cedric Watts's* essay "'A Bloody Racist': About Achebe's View of Conrad" (1983), which defended Conrad's position as an important critic of imperialism* and racism. Furthermore, he detected in Achebe's text an insinuation that white readers are incapable on racial grounds from adequately judging the text. For Watts, this represented a form of inverse racism under the guise of multiculturalism that promotes the kind of racial prejudice that, in his estimation, Conrad's novel sets out to undermine.[4]

Responses

The revised 1988 edition of Achebe's essay shows a very slight modification of his lecture's ferocity: the phrase "bloody racist" is replaced with "thoroughgoing racist." It is unclear whether this is a result of criticism of his lecture or editorial intervention. Later articles, such as "Africa's Tarnished Name" (1998), "African Literature as Restoration of Celebration" (1990), and a number of relatively recent interviews, however, suggest that Achebe's views on Conrad and racism remained largely unchanged.[5] In a 2003 interview with the *Guardian*, for instance, Achebe addresses critics of his work who claim that Conrad's attitudes to race are simply a product of a less progressive era, saying to them: "Great artists manage to be bigger than their times. In the case of Conrad you can actually show that there were people at the same time as him, and before him, who were not racists with regard to Africa."[6]

He also restates one of his original arguments from *An Image of Africa*— that Conrad depicts Africans as lacking humanity—and suggests that there can be no excuses for this mode of characterization: "You cannot compromise my humanity in order that you explore your own ambiguity. I cannot accept that. My humanity is not to be debated, nor is it to be used simply to illustrate European problems."[7]

Conflict and Consensus

While acknowledging the seismic import and influence of Achebe's initial critical inquiry, and agreeing that Conrad's depiction of Africa and Africans displays racist tendencies, most critics tend to arrive at a more moderate view. Such critics, the most significant of whom is probably Patrick Brantlinger,* have attempted to take the historical context into account to stake out a middle ground. While agreeing that *Heart of Darkness* reveals what could be construed as racist views, they point out that the novel also displays relatively progressive opinions for its time on colonialism* and conclude that Conrad is not particularly blameworthy, noting that any condemnation is unfairly based on anachronistic criteria.[8] Such scholars maintain that Conrad disdainfully opposes European imperialism, which was at its height in 1900, and shows sympathy for the plight of Africans. A number of others, including the English literature scholar Jeffrey Williams,* argue that *Heart of Darkness* represents not a real Africa but an allegory of the narrator Charles Marlow's* individual psychological descent.[9]

Although no clear critical consensus has been reached on the contentious issue of Conrad's racism in *Heart of Darkness*, on the whole Achebe has been in the minority with his vehement and provocative views on racism in the novel.

NOTES

1   Ezenwa-Oheato, *Chinua Achebe: A Biography* (Oxford: James Currey, 1997), 191.

2   Chinua Achebe, *Hopes and Impediments: Selected Essays* (New York: Doubleday, 1989), x.

3   See Susan Blake, "Racism and the Classics: Teaching *Heart of Darkness*," *College Language Association Journal* 25, no. 4 (1982), 396–404; Benita Parry, *Conrad and Imperialism* (London: Macmillan, 1983); Eugene B. Redmond, "Racism or Realism? Literary Apartheid or Poetic License? Conrad's Burden in *The Nigger of the Narcissus*," in Joseph Conrad, *The Nigger of the Narcissus*, ed. Robert Kimbrough (New York: Norton, 1979), 358–368; Bette London, "Reading Race and Gender in Conrad's Dark Continent," *Criticism* 31, no. 3 (1989), 235–252.

4   Cedric Watts, "'A Bloody Racist': About Achebe's View of Conrad," *Yearbook of English Studies* 13 (1983), 196–209.

5   Chinua Achebe, "Viewpoint," *Times Literary Supplement,* February 1, 1980; Caryl Phillips, "Out of Africa," *Guardian*, February 22, 2003.

6   Phillips, "Out of Africa."

7   Phillips, "Out of Africa."

8   Patrick Brantlinger, *Rule of Darkness: British Literature and Imperialism, 1830–1914* (New York: Cornell University Press, 1988).

9   Jeffrey Williams, *Theory and the Novel* (Cambridge: Cambridge University Press, 1998).

MODULE 10
THE EVOLVING DEBATE

KEY POINTS

- The publication of "An Image of Africa" opened up a vigorous and ongoing debate about the supposed racist and colonialist* views of Joseph Conrad* (and other nineteenth-century writers).

- Achebe's text, which pivotally impacted studies of Conrad, is also recognized as an important and pioneering work of postcolonial* criticism.

- Contemporary literary critics working on Conrad, or on late-Victorian literature more broadly, continue to assess, analyze, and take issue with Achebe's reading of Conrad's racism.

Uses and Problems

With "An Image of Africa: Racism in Conrad's *Heart of Darkness*," Chinua Achebe became the first critic to challenge the critical consensus regarding Joseph Conrad's novel *Heart of Darkness*. Achebe's impact upon the evolution of Conrad criticism thus cannot be overstated. Its publication began a forceful critical argument, which is still taking place, about whether Conrad (and other nineteenth-century writers) ignores, defends, or propagates racist and colonialist views.

In his introduction to the Norton critical edition of *Heart of Darkness*, the Conrad scholar Robert Kimbrough* calls Achebe's essay one of "the three most important events in *Heart of Darkness* criticism."[1] Kimbrough's edition of the novel gives a good sense of the ensuing debate on racism that was sparked immediately after Achebe's essay, not least by reprinting "An Image of Africa" alongside Wilson Harris's* "The Frontier on Which *Heart of Darkness Stands*" (1981),

> **❝** Achebe's essay ... is, therefore, in the light of Western malaise and post-imperial hangover, a persuasive argument, but I am convinced his judgment or dismissal of *Heart of Darkness*—and of Conrad's strange genius—is a profoundly mistaken one. **❞**
>
> Wilson Harris, "The Frontier on Which *Heart of Darkness* Stands"

Frances B Singh's* "The Colonialist Bias of *Heart of Darkness*" (1978), and C. P. Sarvan's "Racism and the *Heart of Darkness*" (1980). Of these critics, Harris and Sarvan defend Conrad, arguing that while Conrad's language opens him up to charges of racism, ultimately *Heart of Darkness* is critical of colonialism so cannot be considered a racist text. By contrast, Singh agrees with Achebe (although not in such strong terms) that Conrad's novel is infused with racist and colonialist biases.

In the wake of questions raised by Achebe's essay and his work more broadly, classic works of literature continue to be reevaluated for their depictions of race, and processes of recuperation are continuing in order to rehabilitate forgotten or overlooked works of literature by black and other minority authors. "An Image of Africa" has proved so influential that it has now become a mainstream perspective on Conrad's work and a key work of literary criticism, taught in universities alongside *Heart of Darkness* and on courses that survey the development of literary theory.

Schools of Thought

Beyond its impact on studies of Conrad, Achebe's essay (and the questions it raises) has helped shape *postcolonial theory and criticism. Postcolonial theory has played an important role in shaping* literary and cultural criticism since the 1980s, supporting Achebe's broad rejection of the validity of a literary canon* that spreads racist or Orientalist values. It also follows Achebe in questioning the validity and authority of the Western canon, which traditionally has not contained works by authors outside Western culture or given voice to non-Western perspectives of colonialism. Contemporary postcolonial literary critics are also answering Achebe's call to broaden the literary canon and expand the types of work considered worthy of critical inquiry.

Following Achebe's lead, feminist and gender critics such as Johanna M. Smith* and Nina Pelikan Strauss have reinterpreted the novel as one that not only belittles black Africans but also women.[2] On the whole, though, while almost all literary critics acknowledge the importance of Achebe's argument and agree with his claim that Conrad's views are open to accusations of racism, most believe that Achebe's position is too radical.

In Current Scholarship

In addition to inspiring individual followers, Achebe's "An Image of Africa" represents a pedagogical shift in literary studies (that is, a change in the way that literary studies are taught). According to this shift, narratives emerging from outside the perimeters of an Anglophone (English-speaking) tradition can be reclaimed from a negative and Eurocentric* perspective and be assessed on their own merits. As a result, postcolonial critics have developed questions about representations of race raised by Achebe's essay. For instance, in *Culture and Imperialism* (1993), Edward Said* points out that, in the British novelist Jane Austen's* *Mansfield Park* (1814), the material wealth of the heroine comes from an Antiguan sugar plantation maintained by slave labor. For Said, the fact that Austen does not acknowledge or engage with the issue of slavery means that the novel does nothing to "prevent or inhibit or give resistance to horrendously unattractive imperialist* practices" and, then, in some ways condones these practices.[3] In this way, Said's argument correlates strongly with Achebe's assertion that much of Western canonical literature contains prejudice and bias that readers have failed to question and criticize for too long.

NOTES

1   Ezenwa-Oheato, *Chinua Achebe: A Biography* (Oxford: James Currey, 1997), 259.

2   See Johanna M. Smith, "'Too Beautiful Altogether': Patriarchal Ideology in *Heart of Darkness*," in Joseph Conrad, *Heart of Darkness: A Case Study in Contemporary Criticism,* ed. Ross C. Murfin (New York: St. Martin's, 1989), 179–195; Nina Pelikan Straus, "The Exclusion of the Intended from Secret Sharing," in *Joseph Conrad*, ed. Elaine Jordan, (New York: St Martin, 1996), 48–66.

3   Edward Said, *Culture and Imperialism* (London: Random House, 1994), 97.

MODULE 11
IMPACT AND INFLUENCE TODAY

KEY POINTS

- Achebe's text has inspired reinterpretations of classic works like Conrad's *Heart of Darkness* from postcolonial,* feminist,* new historicist,* and queer* perspectives— all "revisionist" approaches challenging orthodox assumptions.

- Defenses of Conrad* made by critics from developing nations have highlighted the difficulty of forming unbiased critical readings.

- Edward Said* is critical of Achebe's personal approach, suggesting that it would be more helpful to develop a comparative and unbiased reading of colonial literature.

Position

Chinua Achebe's "An Image of Africa: Racism in Conrad's *Heart of Darkness*" sparked off critical debates over imperialism* and racism in *Heart of Darkness* that still continue. Today the essay remains relevant as an essential contribution to Conrad studies as well as a foundational text in literary and postcolonial theory. Since it is now taught in universities alongside *Heart of Darkness,* and on courses that offer an introduction to literary theory, the essay continues to reach new critics and readers, and has the potential to make a lasting impact on literary studies.

In terms of broader contemporary relevance, Achebe's essay is also preoccupied with the idea that it is wrong for Conrad's novel to be considered an example of "permanent literature" (what we might call canonical* literature).[1] Achebe's focus on the context of the novel rather than simply the text itself has inspired challenging readings from

> ❝ Like many other readers, I have long regarded *Heart of Darkness* as one of the greatest works of fiction, and have felt that part of its greatness lies in the power of its criticisms of racial prejudice. ❞
>
> Cedric Watts, "'A Bloody Racist': About Achebe's View of Conrad"

a range of theoretical perspectives: postcolonial, feminist, new historicist (criticism that specifically accounts for the historical context of author and critic) and queer (criticism that offers reading of texts that emphasizes places where normative heterosexual categories are unsettled or subverted). All have continued Achebe's task of uncovering racist, sexist, homophobic, or other negative values in works of classic or canonical literature. Rather than attacking the authors of such works with racism or prejudice, however, contemporary literary critics use such texts to evaluate the dominance of certain views at particular historical moments.

Interaction

Although many critics defended Conrad against Achebe's charges of racism, perhaps those who were most challenged by it were other writers and thinkers who had similarly suffered the kind of systematic discrimination Achebe had known in his youth in colonial Nigeria. This difference between "first world" and "third world" interpretations (interpretations made by critics from developed and so-called developing nations) makes clear the problems of assessing Achebe's position. This is particularly the case among those third-world commentators who contend that the novel is critical of the underlying racist attitudes supporting European imperialism.

For instance, while C. P. Sarvan of the University of Zambia acknowledges the legitimacy of Achebe's concern, he concludes that "Conrad reflects to some degree the attitudes of his age, and his description of the fireman as a dog in a parody of breeches, is cruel." He continues, "It is extreme to say that Conrad called into question the very humanity of the African, one's perspective and evaluation of this work need alteration."[2] Similarly, the British Caribbean playwright and essayist Caryl Phillips* has observed, "I disagree with Achebe's response to the novel and have never viewed Conrad—as Achebe states in his lecture—as simply a thorough-going racist."[3] Criticisms like these highlight that interpretations of Conrad cannot simply be divided into Western responses, which unconsciously or not support what Achebe sees as Conrad's racist view, and responses in the developing world, which might be expected to support Achebe's argument. They also make clear the difficulty, perhaps impossibility, of objectivity and impartiality in any assessment of *Heart of Darkness*.

The Contemporary Debate

Achebe is not the only writer concerned with overcoming negative images of formerly colonized societies. Edward Said* declared a similar aim in his celebrated *Orientalism* (1978): "My hope is to illustrate the formidable structure of cultural domination and, specifically for formerly colonized peoples, the dangers and temptations of employing this structure upon themselves or upon others."[4] Said's argument likewise begins with a negative premise that presents the "Other" as the key reference point by which one's identity is defined. The idea of the "Orient," like Achebe's Africa, is a projected scapegoat through which "European culture gained in strength and identity by setting itself off against the Orient as a sort of surrogate and ever underground self."[5]

Surprisingly, Said is critical of Achebe's reading of Conrad. In *Culture and Imperialism* (1993), Said indicates that *Heart of Darkness* is nothing short of a "literary institution" and contests Achebe's overly aggressive condemnation, suggesting that it is couched in an unhelpful "rhetoric of blame." [6] For Said, it is more important to transcend one's implication in the ideological messages transmitted by texts such as *Heart of Darkness* in order to reread them critically as part of a wider genre of imperialist fiction.

For Said, Achebe's approach is misguided. Said is concerned not so much with demonstrating the untruthfulness of European images of formerly colonial societies but in identifying them merely as discourses. Only from this point—from understanding the reductive images they communicate as language—can their systems and consequently their power, be effectively deconstructed.

NOTES

1   Chinua Achebe, "An Image of Africa: Racism in Conrad's *Heart of Darkness*," *Massachusetts Review* 18, no. 4 (1977): 783.

2   C. P. Sarvan, "Racism and the *Heart of Darkness*," International Fiction Review 7, no.1 (1980).

3   Caryl Phillips, quoted in Joseph Conrad, *Heart of Darkness: A Case Study in Contemporary Criticism*, ed. Ross C. Murfin (New York: St. Martin's, 1989), 132.

4   Edward Said, *Orientalism* (New York: Random House, 1979), 25.

5   Said, *Orientalism*, 3.

6   Edward Said, *Culture and Imperialism* (London: Random House, 1994), 97, 18.

MODULE 12
WHERE NEXT?

KEY POINTS

- Debates over the arguments presented within "An Image of Africa" look set to continue, as no critical consensus has been arrived at regarding the contentious issue of Joseph Conrad's* racism in *Heart of Darkness*.

- The text will certainly continue to be taught alongside Conrad's novel in order to illustrate the complex relations between classic literary texts and imperial* or racial ideology.

- Largely because "An Image of Africa" constituted an entirely new and original way of approaching Conrad's famed novel, the text is today considered one of the most important works of literary criticism of the twentieth century.

Potential

Chinua Achebe's "An Image of Africa: Racism in Conrad's *Heart of Darkness*" remains influential. Achebe's critique of Joseph Conrad is currently recognized as one of the most provocative interventions on late-Victorian literature (literature from the end of the nineteenth century). Debates look set to continue, as no outright critical consensus has been achieved on the issue of Conrad's supposed racism in *Heart of Darkness*. Criticism of the extremity of Achebe's viewpoint in "An Image of Africa" has certainly not diminished the essay's status or relevance as a significant work of postcolonial* literary criticism and a key work of Conrad criticism. Indeed, few contemporary literary-studies scholars would dispute the current influence of Achebe's initial critical inquiry, or the likelihood that it will continue

> ❝Achebe is, of course, the best known of African authors, with his first novel, *Things Fall Apart,* having sold several million copies in English and been translated into more than a dozen languages, including several African languages.❞
>
> Stewart Brown, "Reviewed Work: *Chinua Achebe: A Biography* by Ezenwa-Ohaeoto"

to be taught alongside Conrad's novel in order to illustrate the complex relations between classic literary texts and imperial or racial ideology.

Beyond its impact on studies of Conrad and literary studies in general, Achebe's essay continues to influence postcolonial literary critics. Indeed, developing from questions about representations of race raised by Achebe's essay, postcolonial critics continue to undertake important work reevaluating depictions of race in classic and popular works of literature.

In consequence, it is clear that "An Image of Africa" has managed to attain enduring relevance—and there are no signs that this will soon change.

Future Directions

Although there are no particularly committed disciples of "An Image of Africa" in literary studies and postcolonial criticism today, nevertheless scholars in both fields continue to be inspired by its arguments. Achebe's essay also appears likely to continue to influence future literary critics—considering, for example, that it is frequently taught in universities alongside *Heart of Darkness.*

Furthermore, the essay looks set to be considered a text that should be read and discussed by the general public. In 2010 the publisher Penguin included the essay in its "Great Ideas" series, a collection of important and influential texts that are "the works of the great thinkers, pioneers, radicals and visionaries whose ideas shook civilization, and helped make us who we are"—works which "changed the world" and "inspired debate, dissent, war and revolution."[1] Achebe's essay features alongside a variety of seminal texts, ranging from "Of Human Freedom" by the second century Greco-Roman philosopher Epictetus* to "Hosts of Living Forms," extracts from the pioneering evolutionary naturalist Charles Darwin's* *On the Origin of Species* (1859). In 2011 "An Image of Africa" was also included in the *Guardian's* list of the 100 greatest nonfiction books of all time.

Summary

Achebe's critique of *Heart of Darkness* deserves special attention as it is now considered one of the most important works of literary criticism of the twentieth century. "An Image of Africa" constituted an entirely original way of approaching Conrad's celebrated novel. Indeed, with the lecture and published essay, Achebe became the first critic to challenge forcefully the critical consensus that *Heart of Darkness* was an important anti-colonialist text. Instead Achebe argued that though *Heart of Darkness* may be critical of colonialism* it is also inherently racist in the ways that it depicts African natives. At the time of his lecture, Achebe's focus on Conrad's portrayal of natives as savage and inhuman was unique. Also revolutionary was the related question of whether a novel that espouses racist attitudes should be considered a great work of art and worthy of canonical* status. These arguments challenged the orthodoxy surrounding *Heart of Darkness*—as they continue to do today. However, Achebe's work has also gone beyond analysis of Conrad and has inspired students and academics to investigate prejudices and biases within the Western canon more generally.

NOTES

1 "Penguin Great Ideas," accessed February 20, 2013, http://www.penguin.co.uk/static/cs/uk/0/minisites/greatideas/index.html.

GLOSSARY

GLOSSARY OF TERMS

Algerian War: also called Algerian War of Independence (1954–62), in which the National Liberation Front began a war for Algerian independence from France, seeking recognition at the UN to establish a sovereign Algerian state.

Benin Massacre: the defeat of a British expedition in 1897 looking for ivory in Benin, which was met with heavy resistance and left only two British soldiers alive.

Biafra: a secessionist state of Nigeria, in existence from 1967 to 1970. During this time, the Nigerian Civil War—also known as the Biafran War—was fought between the Biafran secessionists and the Nigerian state, in which an estimated one to three million civilians were killed.

Black nationalism: a social and political movement—especially prominent during the 1960s and 1970s—that advocates the principles of unity and self-determination for those who associate themselves with a black identity.

Canon: a Western or European literary canon is the body of literature considered by scholars to be worthy of academic study and criticism.

Colonialism: a social, political, and economic phenomenon by which several European nations established control over nations in other parts of the world.

Cubism: a movement in the arts in the beginning of the twentieth century that combined views of the same subject presented from a variety of different angles. Representative figures include Pablo Picasso and Georges Braque.

Decolonization: the dissolution of the process of colonialism. There have been various waves of decolonization, principally following World War II as a response to a growing desire for independence from colonized states on seeing that European colonial powers could be toppled.

Eurocentric: a term that describes a focus on Europe, its peoples, institutions, and cultures at the expense of other nations or cultures.

Feminism: a movement that began in the nineteenth century with what is known as first-wave feminism, which was largely concerned with voting rights for women. Second-wave feminism began in the late 1960s and lasted until the early 1980s, focusing upon issues such as the woman's place within the family, workplace, and so on.

Feminist criticism: a type of criticism that explores texts and cultural artifacts with the goal of locating and exploring ways in which women have been systematically excluded and oppressed by male-dominated societies.

Gay rights movement: also referred to as the gay liberation movement, a group that was active predominantly throughout the late 1960s to the early 1980s, in numerous Western countries. The movement focused upon encouraging lesbian women and gay men to participate in gay pride, through such measures as coming out to friends and family, taking part in gay pride marches, and so on.

Hegemony: predominant influence, as of a state, region, or group, over another or others.

Igbo: an indigenous ethnic group from Nigeria.

Imperialism: the policy of extending a nation or empire's rule or authority over another territory by means of territorial acquisition and political and economic dominance. Various European powers have extensively practiced imperialism, usually through colonization. It was especially common during the nineteenth and early-to-mid-twentieth centuries.

Modernism: a cultural movement that came into existence during the mid-to-late-nineteenth century, and which had a profound impact on art and thought in Europe and America. Modernism is best understood as a culture—or a series of ideas, beliefs, and values—that rebelled against ideals (largely derived from the ancient world) that had underpinned Western art since the Renaissance.

New Criticism: a formalist movement that emphasized "close reading" (close focus and analysis) of texts. It was popular in American literary criticism in the mid-twentieth century.

New Historicism: a literary theory first developed in the 1980s. It revolved around the idea that literature should be understood and studied within the context of the history of both the author and critic.

Orientalism: a term referring to Western interpretations of the institutions, cultures, arts, and social life of countries of the Far and Middle East. It is often used today with reference to the study of stereotyping and prejudice against Islamic societies.

Postcolonial criticism: a theoretical movement that developed in the 1970s concerned with narratives emerging from the "third world." Specifically, postcolonial theorists look at the ways literature and culture produced by artists from formerly colonized territories transmit codes of power in relation to notions of colonial hegemony. Representative figures include Edward Said and Gayatri Spivak.

Psychoanalysis: a theory developed in the late-nineteenth century by Austrian neurologist Sigmund Freud (1856–1939).

Queer theory: a theory that tries to read texts with an eye to exploring places where normative heterosexual categories are unsettled or subverted. It is closely related to gay and lesbian studies, but also influenced by poststructural theory.

Vietnam War: a conflict in South Vietnam from 1955 to 1975, waged first by France and subsequently by the United States where it sparked large-scale civil protests. By 1970 the majority of Americans believed that it had been a mistake to send troops to Vietnam and the last US troops were withdrawn in 1973.

PEOPLE MENTIONED IN THE TEXT

Jane Austen (1775–1817) was a British novelist whose romantic fiction—works such as *Sense and Sensibility*, *Pride and Prejudice*, and *Mansfield Park*—has made her one of the most widely read British writers.

Patrick Brantlinger (b. 1941) is James Rudy Professor Emeritus at Indiana University Bloomington. His research focuses on Victorian studies and postcolonial studies.

Charlotte Brontë (1816–55) was an English novelist and poet, and one of the three Brontë sisters. She is ranked among the most famous Victorian authors and is best known for her novel *Jane Eyre* (1847).

Joyce Cary (1888–1957) was an Anglo-Irish novelist who wrote frequently on West Africa following his experience in the colonial service, which took him to Nigeria where he held several posts.

Joseph Conrad (1857–1924) was a Polish immigrant to England who wrote a number of novels and essays. His work is considered an important early example of modernist writing. His significant novels include *Lord Jim* (1900) and *Nostromo* (1904).

Charles Darwin (1809–82) was a British naturalist, most famous for his work on evolutionary theory, and specifically for developing the theory of natural selection, the belief that all animals are descended from a common ancestor.

André Derain (1880–1954) was a French artist and sculptor, and a key figure in the Fauvist movement.

Epictetus (c. 55–135 B.C.E.) was a Greco-Roman philosopher. He is known for his writing on Stoic ethics.

Frantz Fanon (1925–61) was a French Martiniquais psychiatrist and writer, whose work was influential in the field of postcolonial studies.

Dorian Gray is the fictional protagonist of *The Picture of Dorian Gray* (1891), a novel by Oscar Wilde that tells the story of a handsome young man who sells his soul in order to retain his youth and beauty, while his portrait bears the marks of his life of debauchery.

Wilson Harris (b. 1921) is a Guyanese writer, best known for his poetry, novels, and essays. He is considered one of the most influential Caribbean artists and experts on postwar literature in English.

Hunt Hawkins (b. 1943) is professor and department chair of English at the University of South Florida, and was former president of the Joseph Conrad Society.

Robert Kimbrough is professor emeritus of English at the University of Wisconsin-Madison. Kimbrough served as editor of the Norton Critical Editions of *Heart of Darkness*.

F. R. Leavis (1895–1978) was an extremely influential critic based at Cambridge University who played a key role in defining the field of English literature as an academic discipline. He founded and edited the academic journal *Scrutiny*.

Bette London is professor of English at the University of Rochester, where her research focuses on authorship in the context of nineteenth- and twentieth-century British writing.

Henri Matisse (1869–1954) was a leading figure in early-twentieth-century modern art and a founder of the Fauvist movement, a group of artists whose work emphasized strong color rather than realism. The French painter's work was characterized by its use of bold and expressive color.

Albert Memmi (b. 1920) is a Tunisian Jewish writer and critic whose works explore the psychological effects of colonialism on colonizers and colonized.

Peter Nazareth (b. 1940) is a Ugandan-born professor of English and African American world studies at the University of Iowa. He is a well-known writer and critic of fiction and drama.

Benita Parry is professor emeritus in English and comparative literary studies at the University of Warwick. Her research interests include the literature of colonialism, imperialism, and postcolonial studies.

Caryl Phillips (b. 1958) is a Kittitian British playwright, novelist, and essayist. He is best known for his novels *The Final Passage* (1985) and *Crossing the River* (1993).

Pablo Picasso (1881–1973) was a Spanish painter and sculptor, one of the most influential artists of the twentieth century, widely known for being one of the founders of the Cubist movement.

Eugene B. Redmond (b. 1937) is an American academic and poet. He is emeritus professor of English at Southern Illinois University Edwardsville, and writes poetry connected to the Black Arts Movement in St. Louis, Illinois.

Jean Rhys (1890–1979) was a writer from the Caribbean island of Dominica. She is best known for her postcolonial novel *Wide Sargasso Sea* (1966).

Edward Said (1935–2003) was a Palestinian American literary theorist and a founding figure in the field of postcolonial studies.

Leopold Senghor (1906–2001) was a Senegalese cultural theorist, poet, and politician who served as president of Senegal between 1960 and 1980.

Frances B. Singh is professor of English in Hostos Community College in the South Bronx district of New York City.

Johanna M. Smith is associate professor of English at the University of Texas at Arlington. Her teaching and research focuses upon drama, law, and literature, particularly eighteenth- and nineteenth-century British literature.

Gayatri Chakravorty Spivak (b. 1942) is an Indian literary and cultural theorist based in the United States. She has written extensively on colonialism, women, and power. Her most widely read essay is "Can the Subaltern Speak?" (1988).

Ngugi wa Thiong'o (b. 1938) is distinguished professor in the departments of comparative literature and English at the University of California, Irvine. He is both a novelist and theorist, particularly of postcolonial literature.

Maurice de Vlaminck (1876–1958) was a French painter. Along with Derain and Matisse, he is considered to be one of the key exponents of the Fauvist movement.

Cedric Watts is emeritus professor of English at the University of Sussex, and a well-known expert on Conrad (among other staple literary figures such as Shakespeare and Keats).

Jeffrey Williams (b. 1958) is professor of English at Carnegie Mellon University. Williams studies and teaches about the novel, in particular contemporary American fiction, as well as literary criticism and theory.

WORKS CITED

WORKS CITED

Achebe, Chinua. *The Education of a British-Protected Child*. London: Penguin, 2011.

"An Image of Africa: Racism in Conrad's *Heart of Darkness*." *Massachusetts Review* 18, no.4 (1977): 782–794.

Hopes and Impediments: Selected Essays. New York: Doubleday, 1989.

Morning Yet on Creation Day: Essays. London: Anchor, 1975.

"Viewpoint." *Times Literary Supplement*, February 1, 1980.

Blake, Susan. "Racism and the Classics: Teaching *Heart of Darkness*." *College Language Association Journal* 25, no. 4 (1982): 396–404.

Brantlinger, Patrick. *Rule of Darkness: British Literature and Imperialism, 1830–1914*. New York: Cornell University Press, 1988.

Brown, Stewart. "Reviewed Work: *Chinua Achebe: A Biography* by Ezenwa-Ohaeoto." *African Affairs* 98, no. 392 (1999): 433–434.

Clifford, James. *The Predicament of Culture*. Cambridge, MA: Harvard University Press, 1988.

Conrad, Joseph. *Heart of Darkness: A Case Study in Contemporary Criticism*. Edited by Ross C. Murfin. New York: St. Martin's, 1989.

Heart of Darkness and Other Tales. Edited by Cedric Watts. London: Oxford World's Classics, 2008.

Duerden, Dennis, and Cosmo Pieterse, eds. *African Writers Talking: A Collection of Interviews*. London: Heinemann, 1972.

Ezenwa-Oheato. *Chinua Achebe: A Biography*. Oxford: James Currey, 1997.

Hawkins, Hunt. "The Issue of Racism in *Heart of Darkness*." *Conradiana* 14, no.3 (1982): 163–171.

Hay, Eloise Knapp. *The Political Novels of Joseph Conrad*. Chicago: Chicago University Press, 1963.

Kettle, Arnold. *An Introduction to the English Novel*. Vol. 2. London: Hutchinson, 1953.

London, Bette. "Reading Race and Gender in Conrad's Dark Continent." *Criticism* 31, no.3 (1989): 235–252.

Parry, Benita. *Conrad and Imperialism.* London: Macmillan, 1983.

"Penguin Great Ideas." Accessed February 20, 2013. http://www.penguin.co.uk/static/cs/uk/0/minisites/greatideas/index.html.

Phillips, Caryl. "Out of Africa." *Guardian.* February 22, 2003.

Redmond, Eugene B. "Racism or Realism? Literary Apartheid or Poetic License? Conrad's Burden in *The Nigger of the Narcissus.*" In Joseph Conrad, *The Nigger of the Narcissus*, edited by Robert Kimbrough, 358–368. New York: Norton, 1979.

Said, Edward. *Culture and Imperialism.* London: Random House, 1994.

Orientalism. New York: Random House, 1979.

Sarvan, C. P. "Racism and the *Heart of Darkness.*" *International Fiction Review* 7, no.1 (1980).

Showalter, Elaine. "Man Booker Prizes: Elaine Showalter Discusses the Work of Chinua Achebe at the Man Booker International Prize in Fiction, June 28, 2007." Accessed May 18, 2015. http://www.themanbookerprize.com/feature/elaine-showalter-discusses-work-chinua-achebe-man-booker-international-prize-fiction-june-28.

Smith, Johanna M. "'Too Beautiful Altogether': Patriarchal Ideology in *Heart of Darkness.*" In Joseph Conrad, *Heart of Darkness: A Case Study in Contemporary Criticism,* edited by Ross C. Murfin, 179–95. New York: St Martin's, 1989.

Spivak, Gayatri Chakravorty. "A Moral Dilemma." In *What Happens to History: The Renewal of Ethics in Contemporary Thought*, edited by Howard Marchitello, 215–237. New York: Routledge, 2001.

Straus, Nina Pelikan. "The Exclusion of the Intended from Secret Sharing." In *Joseph Conrad,* edited by Elaine Jordan, 48-66. New York: St Martin, 1996.

Watts, Cedric. "'A Bloody Racist': About Achebe's View of Conrad." *Yearbook of English Studies* 13 (1983): 196–209.

Williams, Jeffrey. *Theory and the Novel.* Cambridge: Cambridge University Press, 1998.

THE MACAT LIBRARY
BY DISCIPLINE

The Macat Library By Discipline

AFRICANA STUDIES

Chinua Achebe's *An Image of Africa: Racism in Conrad's Heart of Darkness*
W. E. B. Du Bois's *The Souls of Black Folk*
Zora Neale Huston's *Characteristics of Negro Expression*
Martin Luther King Jr's *Why We Can't Wait*
Toni Morrison's *Playing in the Dark: Whiteness in the American Literary Imagination*

ANTHROPOLOGY

Arjun Appadurai's *Modernity at Large: Cultural Dimensions of Globalisation*
Philippe Ariès's *Centuries of Childhood*
Franz Boas's *Race, Language and Culture*
Kim Chan & Renée Mauborgne's *Blue Ocean Strategy*
Jared Diamond's *Guns, Germs & Steel: the Fate of Human Societies*
Jared Diamond's *Collapse: How Societies Choose to Fail or Survive*
E. E. Evans-Pritchard's *Witchcraft, Oracles and Magic Among the Azande*
James Ferguson's *The Anti-Politics Machine*
Clifford Geertz's *The Interpretation of Cultures*
David Graeber's *Debt: the First 5000 Years*
Karen Ho's *Liquidated: An Ethnography of Wall Street*
Geert Hofstede's *Culture's Consequences: Comparing Values, Behaviors, Institutes and Organizations across Nations*
Claude Lévi-Strauss's *Structural Anthropology*
Jay Macleod's *Ain't No Makin' It: Aspirations and Attainment in a Low-Income Neighborhood*
Saba Mahmood's *The Politics of Piety: The Islamic Revival and the Feminist Subject*
Marcel Mauss's *The Gift*

BUSINESS

Jean Lave & Etienne Wenger's *Situated Learning*
Theodore Levitt's *Marketing Myopia*
Burton G. Malkiel's *A Random Walk Down Wall Street*
Douglas McGregor's *The Human Side of Enterprise*
Michael Porter's *Competitive Strategy: Creating and Sustaining Superior Performance*
John Kotter's *Leading Change*
C. K. Prahalad & Gary Hamel's *The Core Competence of the Corporation*

CRIMINOLOGY

Michelle Alexander's *The New Jim Crow: Mass Incarceration in the Age of Colorblindness*
Michael R. Gottfredson & Travis Hirschi's *A General Theory of Crime*
Richard Herrnstein & Charles A. Murray's *The Bell Curve: Intelligence and Class Structure in American Life*
Elizabeth Loftus's *Eyewitness Testimony*
Jay Macleod's *Ain't No Makin' It: Aspirations and Attainment in a Low-Income Neighborhood*
Philip Zimbardo's *The Lucifer Effect*

ECONOMICS

Janet Abu-Lughod's *Before European Hegemony*
Ha-Joon Chang's *Kicking Away the Ladder*
David Brion Davis's *The Problem of Slavery in the Age of Revolution*
Milton Friedman's *The Role of Monetary Policy*
Milton Friedman's *Capitalism and Freedom*
David Graeber's *Debt: the First 5000 Years*
Friedrich Hayek's *The Road to Serfdom*
Karen Ho's *Liquidated: An Ethnography of Wall Street*

John Maynard Keynes's *The General Theory of Employment, Interest and Money*
Charles P. Kindleberger's *Manias, Panics and Crashes*
Robert Lucas's *Why Doesn't Capital Flow from Rich to Poor Countries?*
Burton G. Malkiel's *A Random Walk Down Wall Street*
Thomas Robert Malthus's *An Essay on the Principle of Population*
Karl Marx's *Capital*
Thomas Piketty's *Capital in the Twenty-First Century*
Amartya Sen's *Development as Freedom*
Adam Smith's *The Wealth of Nations*
Nassim Nicholas Taleb's *The Black Swan: The Impact of the Highly Improbable*
Amos Tversky's & Daniel Kahneman's *Judgment under Uncertainty: Heuristics and Biases*
Mahbub Ul Haq's *Reflections on Human Development*
Max Weber's *The Protestant Ethic and the Spirit of Capitalism*

FEMINISM AND GENDER STUDIES

Judith Butler's *Gender Trouble*
Simone De Beauvoir's *The Second Sex*
Michel Foucault's *History of Sexuality*
Betty Friedan's *The Feminine Mystique*
Saba Mahmood's *The Politics of Piety: The Islamic Revival and the Feminist Subject*
Joan Wallach Scott's *Gender and the Politics of History*
Mary Wollstonecraft's *A Vindication of the Rights of Woman*
Virginia Woolf's *A Room of One's Own*

GEOGRAPHY

The Brundtland Report's *Our Common Future*
Rachel Carson's *Silent Spring*
Charles Darwin's *On the Origin of Species*
James Ferguson's *The Anti-Politics Machine*
Jane Jacobs's *The Death and Life of Great American Cities*
James Lovelock's *Gaia: A New Look at Life on Earth*
Amartya Sen's *Development as Freedom*
Mathis Wackernagel & William Rees's *Our Ecological Footprint*

HISTORY

Janet Abu-Lughod's *Before European Hegemony*
Benedict Anderson's *Imagined Communities*
Bernard Bailyn's *The Ideological Origins of the American Revolution*
Hanna Batatu's *The Old Social Classes And The Revolutionary Movements Of Iraq*
Christopher Browning's *Ordinary Men: Reserve Police Batallion 101 and the Final Solution in Poland*
Edmund Burke's *Reflections on the Revolution in France*
William Cronon's *Nature's Metropolis: Chicago And The Great West*
Alfred W. Crosby's *The Columbian Exchange*
Hamid Dabashi's *Iran: A People Interrupted*
David Brion Davis's *The Problem of Slavery in the Age of Revolution*
Nathalie Zemon Davis's *The Return of Martin Guerre*
Jared Diamond's *Guns, Germs & Steel: the Fate of Human Societies*
Frank Dikotter's *Mao's Great Famine*
John W Dower's *War Without Mercy: Race And Power In The Pacific War*
W. E. B. Du Bois's *The Souls of Black Folk*
Richard J. Evans's *In Defence of History*
Lucien Febvre's *The Problem of Unbelief in the 16th Century*
Sheila Fitzpatrick's *Everyday Stalinism*

Eric Foner's *Reconstruction: America's Unfinished Revolution, 1863-1877*
Michel Foucault's *Discipline and Punish*
Michel Foucault's *History of Sexuality*
Francis Fukuyama's *The End of History and the Last Man*
John Lewis Gaddis's *We Now Know: Rethinking Cold War History*
Ernest Gellner's *Nations and Nationalism*
Eugene Genovese's *Roll, Jordan, Roll: The World the Slaves Made*
Carlo Ginzburg's *The Night Battles*
Daniel Goldhagen's *Hitler's Willing Executioners*
Jack Goldstone's *Revolution and Rebellion in the Early Modern World*
Antonio Gramsci's *The Prison Notebooks*
Alexander Hamilton, John Jay & James Madison's *The Federalist Papers*
Christopher Hill's *The World Turned Upside Down*
Carole Hillenbrand's *The Crusades: Islamic Perspectives*
Thomas Hobbes's *Leviathan*
Eric Hobsbawm's *The Age Of Revolution*
John A. Hobson's *Imperialism: A Study*
Albert Hourani's *History of the Arab Peoples*
Samuel P. Huntington's *The Clash of Civilizations and the Remaking of World Order*
C. L. R. James's *The Black Jacobins*
Tony Judt's *Postwar: A History of Europe Since 1945*
Ernst Kantorowicz's *The King's Two Bodies: A Study in Medieval Political Theology*
Paul Kennedy's *The Rise and Fall of the Great Powers*
Ian Kershaw's *The "Hitler Myth": Image and Reality in the Third Reich*
John Maynard Keynes's *The General Theory of Employment, Interest and Money*
Charles P. Kindleberger's *Manias, Panics and Crashes*
Martin Luther King Jr's *Why We Can't Wait*
Henry Kissinger's *World Order: Reflections on the Character of Nations and the Course of History*
Thomas Kuhn's *The Structure of Scientific Revolutions*
Georges Lefebvre's *The Coming of the French Revolution*
John Locke's *Two Treatises of Government*
Niccolò Machiavelli's *The Prince*
Thomas Robert Malthus's *An Essay on the Principle of Population*
Mahmood Mamdani's *Citizen and Subject: Contemporary Africa And The Legacy Of Late Colonialism*
Karl Marx's *Capital*
Stanley Milgram's *Obedience to Authority*
John Stuart Mill's *On Liberty*
Thomas Paine's *Common Sense*
Thomas Paine's *Rights of Man*
Geoffrey Parker's *Global Crisis: War, Climate Change and Catastrophe in the Seventeenth Century*
Jonathan Riley-Smith's *The First Crusade and the Idea of Crusading*
Jean-Jacques Rousseau's *The Social Contract*
Joan Wallach Scott's *Gender and the Politics of History*
Theda Skocpol's *States and Social Revolutions*
Adam Smith's *The Wealth of Nations*
Timothy Snyder's *Bloodlands: Europe Between Hitler and Stalin*
Sun Tzu's *The Art of War*
Keith Thomas's *Religion and the Decline of Magic*
Thucydides's *The History of the Peloponnesian War*
Frederick Jackson Turner's *The Significance of the Frontier in American History*
Odd Arne Westad's *The Global Cold War: Third World Interventions And The Making Of Our Times*

LITERATURE

Chinua Achebe's *An Image of Africa: Racism in Conrad's Heart of Darkness*
Roland Barthes's *Mythologies*
Homi K. Bhabha's *The Location of Culture*
Judith Butler's *Gender Trouble*
Simone De Beauvoir's *The Second Sex*
Ferdinand De Saussure's *Course in General Linguistics*
T. S. Eliot's *The Sacred Wood: Essays on Poetry and Criticism*
Zora Neale Huston's *Characteristics of Negro Expression*
Toni Morrison's *Playing in the Dark: Whiteness in the American Literary Imagination*
Edward Said's *Orientalism*
Gayatri Chakravorty Spivak's *Can the Subaltern Speak?*
Mary Wollstonecraft's *A Vindication of the Rights of Women*
Virginia Woolf's *A Room of One's Own*

PHILOSOPHY

Elizabeth Anscombe's *Modern Moral Philosophy*
Hannah Arendt's *The Human Condition*
Aristotle's *Metaphysics*
Aristotle's *Nicomachean Ethics*
Edmund Gettier's *Is Justified True Belief Knowledge?*
Georg Wilhelm Friedrich Hegel's *Phenomenology of Spirit*
David Hume's *Dialogues Concerning Natural Religion*
David Hume's *The Enquiry for Human Understanding*
Immanuel Kant's *Religion within the Boundaries of Mere Reason*
Immanuel Kant's *Critique of Pure Reason*
Søren Kierkegaard's *The Sickness Unto Death*
Søren Kierkegaard's *Fear and Trembling*
C. S. Lewis's *The Abolition of Man*
Alasdair MacIntyre's *After Virtue*
Marcus Aurelius's *Meditations*
Friedrich Nietzsche's *On the Genealogy of Morality*
Friedrich Nietzsche's *Beyond Good and Evil*
Plato's *Republic*
Plato's *Symposium*
Jean-Jacques Rousseau's *The Social Contract*
Gilbert Ryle's *The Concept of Mind*
Baruch Spinoza's *Ethics*
Sun Tzu's *The Art of War*
Ludwig Wittgenstein's *Philosophical Investigations*

POLITICS

Benedict Anderson's *Imagined Communities*
Aristotle's *Politics*
Bernard Bailyn's *The Ideological Origins of the American Revolution*
Edmund Burke's *Reflections on the Revolution in France*
John C. Calhoun's *A Disquisition on Government*
Ha-Joon Chang's *Kicking Away the Ladder*
Hamid Dabashi's *Iran: A People Interrupted*
Hamid Dabashi's *Theology of Discontent: The Ideological Foundation of the Islamic Revolution in Iran*
Robert Dahl's *Democracy and its Critics*
Robert Dahl's *Who Governs?*
David Brion Davis's *The Problem of Slavery in the Age of Revolution*

The Macat Library By Discipline

Alexis De Tocqueville's *Democracy in America*
James Ferguson's *The Anti-Politics Machine*
Frank Dikotter's *Mao's Great Famine*
Sheila Fitzpatrick's *Everyday Stalinism*
Eric Foner's *Reconstruction: America's Unfinished Revolution, 1863-1877*
Milton Friedman's *Capitalism and Freedom*
Francis Fukuyama's *The End of History and the Last Man*
John Lewis Gaddis's *We Now Know: Rethinking Cold War History*
Ernest Gellner's *Nations and Nationalism*
David Graeber's *Debt: the First 5000 Years*
Antonio Gramsci's *The Prison Notebooks*
Alexander Hamilton, John Jay & James Madison's *The Federalist Papers*
Friedrich Hayek's *The Road to Serfdom*
Christopher Hill's *The World Turned Upside Down*
Thomas Hobbes's *Leviathan*
John A. Hobson's *Imperialism: A Study*
Samuel P. Huntington's *The Clash of Civilizations and the Remaking of World Order*
Tony Judt's *Postwar: A History of Europe Since 1945*
David C. Kang's *China Rising: Peace, Power and Order in East Asia*
Paul Kennedy's *The Rise and Fall of Great Powers*
Robert Keohane's *After Hegemony*
Martin Luther King Jr.'s *Why We Can't Wait*
Henry Kissinger's *World Order: Reflections on the Character of Nations and the Course of History*
John Locke's *Two Treatises of Government*
Niccolò Machiavelli's *The Prince*
Thomas Robert Malthus's *An Essay on the Principle of Population*
Mahmood Mamdani's *Citizen and Subject: Contemporary Africa And The Legacy Of Late Colonialism*
Karl Marx's *Capital*
John Stuart Mill's *On Liberty*
John Stuart Mill's *Utilitarianism*
Hans Morgenthau's *Politics Among Nations*
Thomas Paine's *Common Sense*
Thomas Paine's *Rights of Man*
Thomas Piketty's *Capital in the Twenty-First Century*
Robert D. Putnam's *Bowling Alone*
John Rawls's *Theory of Justice*
Jean-Jacques Rousseau's *The Social Contract*
Theda Skocpol's *States and Social Revolutions*
Adam Smith's *The Wealth of Nations*
Sun Tzu's *The Art of War*
Henry David Thoreau's *Civil Disobedience*
Thucydides's *The History of the Peloponnesian War*
Kenneth Waltz's *Theory of International Politics*
Max Weber's *Politics as a Vocation*
Odd Arne Westad's *The Global Cold War: Third World Interventions And The Making Of Our Times*

POSTCOLONIAL STUDIES

Roland Barthes's *Mythologies*
Frantz Fanon's *Black Skin, White Masks*
Homi K. Bhabha's *The Location of Culture*
Gustavo Gutiérrez's *A Theology of Liberation*
Edward Said's *Orientalism*
Gayatri Chakravorty Spivak's *Can the Subaltern Speak?*

PSYCHOLOGY

Gordon Allport's *The Nature of Prejudice*
Alan Baddeley & Graham Hitch's *Aggression: A Social Learning Analysis*
Albert Bandura's *Aggression: A Social Learning Analysis*
Leon Festinger's *A Theory of Cognitive Dissonance*
Sigmund Freud's *The Interpretation of Dreams*
Betty Friedan's *The Feminine Mystique*
Michael R. Gottfredson & Travis Hirschi's *A General Theory of Crime*
Eric Hoffer's *The True Believer: Thoughts on the Nature of Mass Movements*
William James's *Principles of Psychology*
Elizabeth Loftus's *Eyewitness Testimony*
A. H. Maslow's *A Theory of Human Motivation*
Stanley Milgram's *Obedience to Authority*
Steven Pinker's *The Better Angels of Our Nature*
Oliver Sacks's *The Man Who Mistook His Wife For a Hat*
Richard Thaler & Cass Sunstein's *Nudge: Improving Decisions About Health, Wealth and Happiness*
Amos Tversky's *Judgment under Uncertainty: Heuristics and Biases*
Philip Zimbardo's *The Lucifer Effect*

SCIENCE

Rachel Carson's *Silent Spring*
William Cronon's *Nature's Metropolis: Chicago And The Great West*
Alfred W. Crosby's *The Columbian Exchange*
Charles Darwin's *On the Origin of Species*
Richard Dawkin's *The Selfish Gene*
Thomas Kuhn's *The Structure of Scientific Revolutions*
Geoffrey Parker's *Global Crisis: War, Climate Change and Catastrophe in the Seventeenth Century*
Mathis Wackernagel & William Rees's *Our Ecological Footprint*

SOCIOLOGY

Michelle Alexander's *The New Jim Crow: Mass Incarceration in the Age of Colorblindness*
Gordon Allport's *The Nature of Prejudice*
Albert Bandura's *Aggression: A Social Learning Analysis*
Hanna Batatu's *The Old Social Classes And The Revolutionary Movements Of Iraq*
Ha-Joon Chang's *Kicking Away the Ladder*
W. E. B. Du Bois's *The Souls of Black Folk*
Émile Durkheim's *On Suicide*
Frantz Fanon's *Black Skin, White Masks*
Frantz Fanon's *The Wretched of the Earth*
Eric Foner's *Reconstruction: America's Unfinished Revolution, 1863-1877*
Eugene Genovese's *Roll, Jordan, Roll: The World the Slaves Made*
Jack Goldstone's *Revolution and Rebellion in the Early Modern World*
Antonio Gramsci's *The Prison Notebooks*
Richard Herrnstein & Charles A Murray's *The Bell Curve: Intelligence and Class Structure in American Life*
Eric Hoffer's *The True Believer: Thoughts on the Nature of Mass Movements*
Jane Jacobs's *The Death and Life of Great American Cities*
Robert Lucas's *Why Doesn't Capital Flow from Rich to Poor Countries?*
Jay Macleod's *Ain't No Makin' It: Aspirations and Attainment in a Low Income Neighborhood*
Elaine May's *Homeward Bound: American Families in the Cold War Era*
Douglas McGregor's *The Human Side of Enterprise*
C. Wright Mills's *The Sociological Imagination*

The Macat Library By Discipline

Thomas Piketty's *Capital in the Twenty-First Century*
Robert D. Putman's *Bowling Alone*
David Riesman's *The Lonely Crowd: A Study of the Changing American Character*
Edward Said's *Orientalism*
Joan Wallach Scott's *Gender and the Politics of History*
Theda Skocpol's *States and Social Revolutions*
Max Weber's *The Protestant Ethic and the Spirit of Capitalism*

THEOLOGY

Augustine's *Confessions*
Benedict's *Rule of St Benedict*
Gustavo Gutiérrez's *A Theology of Liberation*
Carole Hillenbrand's *The Crusades: Islamic Perspectives*
David Hume's *Dialogues Concerning Natural Religion*
Immanuel Kant's *Religion within the Boundaries of Mere Reason*
Ernst Kantorowicz's *The King's Two Bodies: A Study in Medieval Political Theology*
Søren Kierkegaard's *The Sickness Unto Death*
C. S. Lewis's *The Abolition of Man*
Saba Mahmood's *The Politics of Piety: The Islamic Revival and the Feminist Subject*
Baruch Spinoza's *Ethics*
Keith Thomas's *Religion and the Decline of Magic*

COMING SOON

Chris Argyris's *The Individual and the Organisation*
Seyla Benhabib's *The Rights of Others*
Walter Benjamin's *The Work Of Art in the Age of Mechanical Reproduction*
John Berger's *Ways of Seeing*
Pierre Bourdieu's *Outline of a Theory of Practice*
Mary Douglas's *Purity and Danger*
Roland Dworkin's *Taking Rights Seriously*
James G. March's *Exploration and Exploitation in Organisational Learning*
Ikujiro Nonaka's *A Dynamic Theory of Organizational Knowledge Creation*
Griselda Pollock's *Vision and Difference*
Amartya Sen's *Inequality Re-Examined*
Susan Sontag's *On Photography*
Yasser Tabbaa's *The Transformation of Islamic Art*
Ludwig von Mises's *Theory of Money and Credit*

Macat Disciplines

Access the greatest ideas and thinkers across entire disciplines, including

Postcolonial Studies

Roland Barthes's *Mythologies*
Frantz Fanon's *Black Skin, White Masks*
Homi K. Bhabha's *The Location of Culture*
Gustavo Gutiérrez's *A Theology of Liberation*
Edward Said's *Orientalism*
Gayatri Chakravorty Spivak's *Can the Subaltern Speak?*

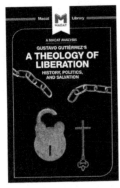

Macat Disciplines

Access the greatest ideas and thinkers across entire disciplines, including

AFRICANA STUDIES

Chinua Achebe's *An Image of Africa: Racism in Conrad's Heart of Darkness*

W. E. B. Du Bois's *The Souls of Black Folk*

Zora Neale Hurston's *Characteristics of Negro Expression*

Martin Luther King Jr.'s *Why We Can't Wait*

Toni Morrison's *Playing in the Dark: Whiteness in the American Literary Imagination*

Macat analyses are available from all good bookshops and libraries.

Access hundreds of analyses through one, multimedia tool.
Join free for one month **library.macat.com**

Macat Disciplines

Access the greatest ideas and thinkers across entire disciplines, including

FEMINISM, GENDER AND QUEER STUDIES

Simone De Beauvoir's
The Second Sex

Michel Foucault's
History of Sexuality

Betty Friedan's
The Feminine Mystique

Saba Mahmood's
*The Politics of Piety:
The Islamic Revival and
the Feminist Subject*

Joan Wallach Scott's
*Gender and the
Politics of History*

Mary Wollstonecraft's
*A Vindication of the
Rights of Woman*

Virginia Woolf's
A Room of One's Own

Judith Butler's
Gender Trouble

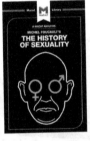

Macat analyses are available from all good bookshops and libraries.

Access hundreds of analyses through one, multimedia tool.

Join free for one month **library.macat.com**

Macat Disciplines
Access the greatest ideas and thinkers across entire disciplines, including

CRIMINOLOGY

Michelle Alexander's
*The New Jim Crow:
Mass Incarceration in the
Age of Colorblindness*

**Michael R. Gottfredson
& Travis Hirschi's**
A General Theory of Crime

Elizabeth Loftus's
Eyewitness Testimony

**Richard Herrnstein
& Charles A. Murray's**
*The Bell Curve: Intelligence and
Class Structure in American Life*

Jay Macleod's
*Ain't No Makin' It:
Aspirations and Attainment in a
Low-Income Neighborhood*

Philip Zimbardo's
The Lucifer Effect

Macat Disciplines

Access the greatest ideas and thinkers across entire disciplines, including

INEQUALITY

Ha-Joon Chang's, *Kicking Away the Ladder*
David Graeber's, *Debt: The First 5000 Years*
Robert E. Lucas's, *Why Doesn't Capital Flow from Rich To Poor Countries?*
Thomas Piketty's, *Capital in the Twenty-First Century*
Amartya Sen's, *Inequality Re-Examined*
Mahbub Ul Haq's, *Reflections on Human Development*

Macat Disciplines

Access the greatest ideas and thinkers across entire disciplines, including

GLOBALIZATION

Arjun Appadurai's, *Modernity at Large: Cultural Dimensions of Globalisation*

James Ferguson's, *The Anti-Politics Machine*

Geert Hofstede's, *Culture's Consequences*

Amartya Sen's, *Development as Freedom*

Macat analyses are available from all good bookshops and libraries.

Access hundreds of analyses through one, multimedia tool.
Join free for one month **library.macat.com**

Printed in the United States
by Baker & Taylor Publisher Services